Dow Theory for the 21st Century

Dow Theory for the 21st Century

TECHNICAL INDICATORS FOR IMPROVING YOUR INVESTMENT RESULTS

Jack Schannep

WILEY

John Wiley & Sons, Inc.

Published by John Wiley & Sons, Inc., Hoboken, New Jersey
Published simultaneously in Canada

For general information on our other products and services or for technical
support, please contact our Customer Care Department within the United States
at (800) 762-2974, outside the United States at (317) 572-3993 or
fax (317) 572-4002.

Wiley also publishes its books in a variety of electronic formats. Some content that
appears in print may not be available in electronic books. For more information
about Wiley products, visit our web site at www.wiley.com.

Library of Congress Cataloging-in-Publication Data

Schannep, Jack, 1934-
    Dow theory for the 21st century : technical indicators for improving your
  investment results / Jack Schannep.
        p.   cm.
    Includes index.
    ISBN 978-0-470-24059-5 (cloth)
        1. Investment analysis.   2. Stock price forecasting.   3. Speculation.
    I. Title.
    HG4529.S33   2008
    332.63'2042–dc22

                                                          2008006125

Printed in the United States of America
10 9 8 7 6 5 4 3 2 1

*To Helen, the love of my life and my life's partner,
I dedicate this book on the occasion
of our 50th wedding anniversary.*

*To our wonderful and successful family,
Bart and Marcella, Dwight and Christy,
Tim and Mary Beth, and Marie
and Mark Manor.*

*To our eight terrific grandchildren,
Rob and bride Robin, Kayla, Sarah,
Allison and Jack Schannep, and Zach,
Mitch and Brett Manor.*

*To investors everywhere, may your financial
success be increased with the help of the concepts
and indicators from this book.*

Contents

Acknowledgments

Thanks to:

Charles Bassetti, editor and coauthor, *Technical Analysis of Stock Trends*, and Zoe Arey of Taylor & Francis Croup, LLC for permission to use excerpts from the eighth edition.

Dave Garrett, Principal, TimerTrac.com, for monitoring the record of my indicators since 1998.

Mark Hulbert, editor, *Hulbert Financial Digest*, for monitoring the record of my indicators since 2002.

Steve LeCompte, Managing Partner, CXO Advisory Group LLC, for permission to include his "Trading Calendar" and for tracking the record of my newsletter.

Kelly O'Connor, Development Editor, John Wiley & Sons, Inc., for attempting to make a readable book from my writings.

Jim O'Shaughnessy, President, O'Shaughnessy Asset Management, author, *What Works on Wall Street* and others, for suggesting I get in touch with John Wiley & Sons to publish my book.

Stephen Reitmeister, Executive Vice President, Zacks Investment Research, and Jon Knotts for including me in their "Featured Experts" section, where many have been introduced to my newsletter and book.

Bart Schannep, Principal, Schannep Investment Advisors, for his computer and investment knowledge and attempts to edit my early efforts.

Tim Schannep, Vice President, CBIZ Wealth Management and Business Retirement Division, for his efforts on my behalf with publishers and agents.

Mark Shepardson, President, Fraser Publishing Company, for permission to quote liberally from Robert Rhea's *The Dow Theory*.

Stacey Small, Senior Editorial Assistant, John Wiley & Sons, Inc., for help in walking this novice author through the maze of publishing and developing the book's cover.

Johnathan Stein, subscriber and e-mail friend, for producing a number of the charts in the book, a task I was unprepared to undertake on my own.

Ron Surz, President and CEO, PPCA, Inc., for permission to use "History for Common Stocks (Adjusted for Inflation)."

Dr. Gerald Swanson, Professor of Economics, University of Arizona, author, *America the Broke* and others, a personal friend, for giving me advice on dealing with a publisher.

Aaron Task, Correspondent, Yahoo! TechTicker, formerly Editor at Large, TheStreet.com, and **Jordan Goldstein,** Vice President, for permission to include "Dow Theory: It's Alive! Alive! And Bullish!"

Introduction:
The What and Why of this Book

A person watching the tide coming in and who wishes to know
the exact spot which marks the high tide, sets a stick in the sand
at the points reached by the incoming waves until the stick
reaches a position where the waves do not come up to it, and
finally recede enough to show that the tide has turned. This
method holds good in watching and determining the flood tide
of the stock market.

Charles H. Dow wrote those words over 100 years ago on
January 31, 1901, and they are as true for the twenty-first century
as they proved to be for the twentieth century. No book on the Dow
Theory should start or finish without his classic quotation, as it is the
very essence of the theory. For the record, the rest of the quote that
appeared in the *Wall Street Journal* that day continued: "The average of twenty stocks is the peg which marks the height of the waves.
The price-waves, like those of the sea, do not recede at once from
the top. The force which moves them checks the inflow gradually
and time elapses before it can be told with certainty whether high
tide has been seen or not."

I wrote this book so that a serious investor will be able to find
almost all he or she needs to know about the stock market and how
to become financially successful in one place. I don't pretend to
know all there is to know about either subject, but I have been an
avid market student and successful personal investor all my professional life. If you have aspirations to know the important things about
the stock market and are not interested in the fluff, then this book is
for you.

You will soon recognize that most of this book is not sexy or even exciting, and some of it may not even be interesting to you, but it contains a wealth of valuable insights, historical precedence, and useful and usable information. I am not a writer by trade, so I apologize up front for any shortcomings in that department. I have spent a lifetime with the stock market, starting in college and extending through a short military career, a full financial business career, and even longer "working" retirement. I started writing a market timing letter to colleagues in the stockbrokerage business in 1977 at the behest of senior officers in my firm, a letter that I continued after I retired. Out of that grew an Internet subscription letter that has attracted subscribers from most of our United States and numerous foreign countries.

The purpose of my market letter and of this book is not to make money personally—the Web site www.TheDowTheory.com is owned by other members of my family who are occasionally surprised by a dividend. My wife and I have been fortunate to have been financially secure for many years, and now it is time to share the "family secrets" with the rest of you.

Do not be afraid to skip over segments of the book (such as the background of Charles Dow or William Peter Hamilton's Editorial, or my own, and other perhaps tedious subjects); you can always come back to them. Concentrate on the big picture and review those areas that don't at first sink in. In the end, I think you will feel much better prepared to face the stock market than ever before. I sincerely hope this book will show you the way to a better understanding of the ingredients that make up the world of finance, specifically the American stock market, and that understanding will lead you further to great investment success.

PART

I

THE TRADITIONAL
DOW THEORY

1

By Way of Background

Every day we hear about the Dow rising or falling and may not stop to think who Dow was and what the Dow Averages are all about. In this chapter, I discuss who Charles Dow was and how his theory, which has served so well for over 100 years, can be used to even better advantage in the twenty-first century as a guide to timing the stock market and making money in it.

How It All Started

Charles Henry Dow was born on a farm in Sterling, Connecticut, in November 1851. At the age of 18, he began his career as a reporter with the *Springfield Republican* and in 1875 moved to the *Providence Journal.* After writing a lengthy study about the transportation systems between Providence and New York City, he developed an interest in business subjects. Young Dow also wrote articles from Leadville, Colorado, on the 1878 silver strike. These articles led directly to his move to New York the next year as a financial reporter for *The New York Mail and Express.*

Subsequently, after he became a writer and editor with the Kiernan News Agency, he hired his friend Edward Jones. Jones had been an editor for the *Providence Sunday Dispatch.* Together, Dow and Jones distributed financial news bulletins to New York's business district. In 1882, bankrolled by another partner, they formed Dow Jones & Company and began publishing the handwritten *Customer's Afternoon Letter,* precursor of the *Wall Street Journal.*

The first stock index published by Dow in 1884 was comprised of 11 stocks, 9 of which were railroads. Five years later, the *Wall Street Journal* first appeared with Dow as editor. It was not until May 26, 1896, that the Dow Jones Industrial Average (DJIA) was born with 12 "smokestack" companies. A year later, a separate average was started to keep track of the railroad stocks (DJTA), which were the primary transportation mode of the day.

Origins and Evolution of the Theory

Dow saw the stock market and his idea, yet to be named by others as Dow's theory, as an indicator of business activity. If business was good, the company's stock would do well. When he spoke of a "person watching the tides," that was, of course, an analogy to the great industrial companies' price movements. To confirm that his reading of the "tides" was correct, he checked another part of the "seashore" to see that the ocean tides were the same there. In the stock market, that meant checking the other index he had created: the railroads, which later became the Transportation Index. Dow had used the two indices in tandem because they were all that was available. The Dow Jones Utilities (DJUA) did not come into existence until 1929; the Standard & Poor's 500 Stock Index (S&P 500), not until 1957.

Dow never explained *why* the two indices—the Industrials and the Transports—*must* confirm; instead he observed that they *did* confirm when their signals subsequently proved to be correct. With the ocean, passing ships or other disruptions can interrupt the ebb and flow, or rogue waves can temporarily upset the determination of the tides rising or falling. By looking in two separate locations along the coast (or in the stock market at a separate industry), Dow believed that it was more likely that the reading would be correct. After all, it is the rails (Transports) that deliver the raw materials, and perhaps even the labor, to the mills of industrial corporations. And in the end, it is the Transports that deliver the finished product to the ultimate consumers. Clearly these two groups are interrelated, just as different areas of a coastline have similar and related tides. So the Industrials and Transports were and still are intertwined and need to be in sync for a proper reading of his theory.

The amazing thing is that Dow only had five years' worth of data on the two averages from which to base his theory. Unfortunately, he had little time to write about and expound on his theory. By 1902, Dow was in failing health and sold the company. He died on December 4 of that year.

Dow never wrote down a complete description of his theory, never dedicated a complete editorial to it, and never gave it a name. A friend, A. J. Nelson, in his *The ABC of Stock Speculation,* named it Dow's theory in 1902. Most of what we know of the theory came from a series of *Wall Street Journal* editorials written by Dow's successor as editor, William Peter Hamilton, between 1902 and 1929. He also wrote about Dow's theory in *The Stock Market Barometer* in 1922.

Rhea's Writings and Hamilton's Quotes

The most organized and thorough description of the Dow Theory as we knew it in the twentieth century came from a book of that name, which was written by Robert Rhea in 1932. My father-in-law had called on Rhea shortly before his death in 1939, and it was through that relationship that I much later developed my interest. Rhea, who was bedridden, had the time and inclination to analyze the 35 years of data available to him to further refine the work of Dow and Hamilton into what I consider the definitive work on the original Dow Theory. The book, which contains both the text by Robert Rhea and selected editorials and quotes by William Peter Hamilton, was reissued in 1993 by Fraser Publishing Company. (Portions are reprinted here with permission.)

Hypotheses

Robert Rhea, after many years of studying the writings of both Dow and Hamilton, set out a "few hypotheses" that he said must be accepted "without reservation whatsoever" if one is to use the theory successfully in order to know when to buy and sell in an effort to make money in the stock market.

1. **Manipulation.** Manipulation is possible in the day-to-day movements of the averages. Secondary reactions are subject to such an influence to a more limited degree, but *the primary trend can never be manipulated.*
2. **Averages discount everything.** The fluctuations of the daily *closing* prices of the Dow-Jones Rail and Industrial averages afford a composite index of all the hopes, disappointments,

and knowledge of everyone who knows anything of financial matters. For that reason, the effects of coming events (excluding acts of God) are always properly anticipated in their movement. The averages quickly appraise such calamities as fires and earthquakes.

3. **The theory is not infallible.** *The Dow Theory is not an infallible system for beating the market.* Its successful use as an aid in speculation requires serious study, and the summing up of evidence must be impartial. The wish must never be allowed to father the thought.

Theorems

The "definite theorems" of the Dow Theory have been rewritten by numerous writers, but I choose to stay with Rhea's book on the Dow Theory, as he actually lived and invested throughout the period that Dow and Hamilton lived. The theorems are altered only to the extent that they are somewhat better organized. After I state the original theorem, I have added notes (identified as "Author's note") in an effort to clarify, expand, and modernize Charles Dow's twentieth-century stock market theory so that it can help investors improve their financial results in the twenty-first century.

Dow's Three Movements

There are three movements of the averages, all of which may be in progress at one and the same time.

1. **The first, and most important, is the primary trend,** which consists of the broad upward or downward movements known as bull or bear markets and may be of several years' duration.

    Primary movements: The *primary movement* is the broad basic trend generally known as a bull or bear market extending over periods that have varied from less than a year to several years. *The most important factor in successful speculation is the correct determination of the direction of this movement. There is no known method of forecasting the extent or duration of a primary movement.*

    Author's note: Once in place, the primary trend is assumed to continue until definitely proven otherwise. This is an offshoot of Isaac Newton's law of physics, which states a body in motion tends to stay in motion unless compelled to change its state.

Primary bear market. *A primary bear market is the long downward movement interrupted by important rallies.* It is caused by various economic ills and does not terminate until stock prices have thoroughly discounted the worst that is apt to occur. A bear market has three principal phases:

   a. Abandonment of the hopes upon which stocks were purchased at inflated prices.
   b. Selling due to decreased business and earnings.
   c. Distress selling of sound securities, regardless of their value, by those who must find a cash market for at least a portion of their assets.

Author's note: These phases go from complacency, to concern, and finally to capitulation, which is covered in detail in Chapter 6.

Primary bull market. *A primary bull market is a broad upward movement, interrupted by secondary reactions, and averaging longer than two years.* During this time, stock prices advance because of a demand created by both investment and speculative buying caused by improving business conditions and increased speculative activity. There are three phases of a bull period:

   a. Reviving confidence in the future of business.
   b. Response of stock prices to known improvement in corporation earnings.
   c. The period when speculation is rampant and inflation apparent—a period when stocks are advanced on hopes and expectations.

2. **The second, and most deceptive movement, is the secondary reaction,** which is an important decline in a primary bull market or a rally in a primary bear market. These reactions *usually last from three weeks to as many months.*

Secondary reaction. For the purpose of this discussion, *a secondary reaction is considered to be an important decline in a bull market or advance in a bear market,* usually lasting from three weeks to as many months, during which intervals the price movement *generally* retraces from 33 percent to 66 percent of the primary price change since the termination of the last preceding secondary reaction. *These reactions are frequently erroneously* *assumed to represent a change of primary trend,* because obviously the first stage of a bull market must always coincide with a movement that might have proved to have been merely a secondary reaction in a bear market, the contra being true after the peak has been attained in a bull market.

Author's note: Many Dow theorists believe the time frame "usually lasting from three weeks to as many months" is cast in stone. Actually, the first reference to the time frame by Dow himself was "from two weeks to a month or more"(December 19, 1900). (Later he wrote: "The secondary movement covers a period ranging from ten days to sixty days" [January 4, 1902]). At various times Hamilton used a time frame for secondary reactions as "extending from 20 days to 60 days [September 17, 1904]," "anywhere from one month to three months [February 26, 1909]," as well as "lasting from a few days to many weeks [February 11, 1922]." It is no wonder that many are confused as to what a secondary reaction is. Actually, these definitions cover a broad area, and the total range of from a few days to three months is correct. My work shows that the minimum time frame can be just days for some signals, but *usually* it is weeks and it can indeed extend for months. The percentage price movement is just a generality and should not be taken as a requirement. After a secondary reaction, the primary trend is *reaffirmed* when *both* the industrials and transports return to extend that trend. In a bull market, such a move to new highs is often described as being "in the clear" and is sometimes labeled as a new buy signal, which is incorrect. The buy signal dates to the original signal. This move merely affirms that signal.

3. **The third, and usually unimportant, movement is the daily fluctuation.** Stocks move up, down, and sideways every day and for the most part those moves are meaningless.

   Daily fluctuations. Inferences drawn from one day's movement of the averages are almost certain to be misleading and are of little value except when "lines" are being formed. The day-to-day movement must be recorded and studied, however, because a series of charted daily movements eventually develops into a pattern that is easily recognized as having a forecasting value.

   Author's note: Lines will be discussed shortly.

Both Averages Must Confirm. The movements of both the Railroad and Industrial stock averages should always be considered together. The movement of *one price average must be confirmed by the other* before reliable inferences may be drawn. Conclusions based on the movement of one average, unconfirmed by the other, are almost certain to prove misleading.

Author's note: A common complaint is that the Railroads (Transports) are of inconsequential import these days, which makes the theory out of date. I would remind the reader that the Transportation Average is actually made up of 20 stocks representing at least *six* industries: airlines, air freight, railroads, rail equipment, marine transport, and trucking. The stocks in the average deliver raw materials and components to industry and then distribute the product to the world. Therefore, their business fortunes are still intertwined.

Determining the Trend. Successive rallies penetrating preceding high points, with ensuing declines terminating above the preceding low points, offer a bullish indication. Conversely, failure of the rallies to penetrate previous high points, with ensuing declines carrying below former low points, is bearish. Such inferences are useful in appraising secondary reactions and are of major importance in forecasting the resumption, continuation, or change of the primary trend. For the purpose of this discussion, *a rally or a decline is one or more daily movements resulting in a net reversal of direction exceeding 3 percent of the price of either average.* Such movements have little authority unless confirmed in direction by both averages, but *confirmation need not occur on the same day.*

Author's note: A modern misconception is that both the Industrials and Transports must make new all-time highs for a bull market to be in force. Some have argued that the 60+ percent gain from the October 2002 lows to the May 2006 high at 11,642.65 was not a bull market because the 2000 all-time high of 11,722.98 was not surpassed. And then in October 2006 it was surpassed, which would imply that those last 80.33 points somehow changed the status to bull market. *A bear market changes to a bull market at the low point,* not *after it gets to a higher point than the last bull market!* Granted, the new bull market is not immediately determinable at that low point, but after a time it can be seen as having been the start. The levels at which a market attains "official" bull or bear market status are covered in Chapters 5 and 6, and you will see that a 60 percent gain over a nearly four-year time frame would certainly qualify as a bull market.

Lines.   A "line" is a price movement extending two to three weeks or longer, during which period the price variation of both averages move within a range of approximately 5 percent. Such a movement indicates either accumulation or distribution. Simultaneous advances above the limits of the line indicate accumulation and predict higher prices; conversely, simultaneous declines below the line imply distribution and lower prices are sure to follow. Conclusions drawn from the movement of one average, not confirmed by the other, generally prove to be incorrect.

Author's note: A line is a period of consolidation, either of accumulation of stocks for an eventual continuation of the bullish trend or of distribution to be followed by a decline. The "break-out" from the range implies further movement in that direction.

Relation of Volume to Price Movements.   A market that has been overbought becomes dull on rallies and develops activity on declines; conversely, when a market is oversold, the tendency is to become dull on declines and active on rallies. Bull markets terminate in a period of excessive activity and begin with comparatively light transactions.

Author's note: New York Stock Exchange (NYSE) volume tends to peak ahead of bull market peaks by an average of about six months, as you will see in Chapter 11.

Double Tops and Double Bottoms.   "Double tops" and "double bottoms" are of little value in forecasting the price movement and have proved to be deceptive more often than not.

Author's note: This is a surprising theorem as I find the "return move" at tops and bottoms to be part of a requirement for Dow Theory signal formation, as you will see in the next chapter. Even though many stock market bottoms take the form of the letter V, a large number are double bottoms; that is, they take the form of the letter W. Likewise, market tops often make twin or double tops, such as the letter M.

Individual Stocks.   All active and well-distributed *stocks of great American corporations generally rally and decline with the averages,* but any individual stock may reflect conditions not applicable to the average price of any diversified list of stocks.

Author's note: This might also be characterized as a rising tide lifts all ships, and a falling tide can sink them. It also brings to mind the subject of index funds, which, of course, did not exist in Rhea's day. They are ideal vehicles for tracking the Standard & Poor's 500 Index (SPY—Spiders), the Dow Jones Industrial Average (DIA—Diamonds), and the NYSE iShares (NYC—no nickname yet, but how about Apples, as in the "Big Apple") will be covered in Chapter 14.

William Peter Hamilton's Most Famous Editorial

Hamilton, the brilliant successor to Charles Dow at the *Wall Street Journal,* wrote this about the "signal for a bear market" on October 25, 1929. (The article is reprinted here with permission.) Unfortunately, Hamilton died two months later, so he never lived to see the prescience of the "call." It is an example of the Dow Theory in action as interpreted at the time.

A Turn in the Tide

On the late Charles H. Dow's well known method of reading the stock market movement from the Dow-Jones averages, the twenty railroad stocks on Wednesday, October 23 confirmed a bearish indication given by the industrials two days before. Together the averages gave the signal for a bear market in stocks after a major bull market with the unprecedented duration of almost six years. It is noteworthy that Barron's and the Dow-Jones NEWS service on October 21 pointed out the significance of the industrial signal, given subsequent confirmation by the railroad average. The comment was as follows:

"If, however, the market broke again, after a failure to pass the old highs, and the decline carried the price of the industrials below 325.17 and the railroads below 168.26, the bearish indication would be strong, and might well represent something more than a secondary reaction, however severe. It has often been said in these studies of the price movement that the barometer never indicates duration. There was a genuine major bear market in 1923, but it lasted only eight months. One good reason for not taking the present indications too seriously is that they have all been recorded in a most unusually short space of time.

The severest reaction from the high point of the year had just one month's duration. In view of the nationwide character of the speculation, this seems a dangerously short period to infer anything like complete reversal in public sentiment."

There was a striking consistency about the market movement since the high figure of September 3. There were at least four rallies in the course of the decline in the industrials before the definite new low point was established and each of these was weaker than the last. Dow always considered this a danger signal, but for the past thirty years it has been the custom in discussing the stock market as a barometer of business to require that one average should confirm the other. Failure to agree has been found deceptive.

There are people trading in Wall Street, and many all over the country who have never seen a real bear market, as for instance, that which began October, 1919, and lasted for two years, or that from 1912 to 1914 which predicted the Great War if the world had then been able to interpret the signs. What is more material is that the stock market does forecast the general business of the country. The big bull market was confirmed by six years of prosperity and if the stock market takes the other direction there will be contraction in business later, although on present indications only in moderate volume.

Some time ago it was said in a *Wall Street Journal* editorial that if the stock market was compelled to deflate, as politicians seemed so earnestly to wish they would shortly after experience a deflation elsewhere which would be much less to their liking.

Not so well known is the editorial from the following day (October 26, 1929), which endorses the Dow Theory signal but also puts a human, and optimistic, face on the situation.

So far as the barometer of the Dow-Jones is concerned it has been clear since last Wednesday (October 23, 1929) that the major movement of the market has turned downwards. The market will find itself, for Wall Street does its own liquidation and always with a remarkable absence of anything like financial catastrophe. Beyond indicating the trend there is no idea here of prediction. *Conditions do not seem to foreshadow anything more formidable than an arrest of stock activity and business prosperity like that in 1923.*

Suggestions that the wiping out of paper profits will reduce the country's real purchasing power seem rather farfetched.

Author's note: I have added italics to emphasize particular points. The 1923 bear market had dropped 18.6 percent over 7.2 months and the recession lasted 14 months, from May 1923 to July 1924. The 1929 bear market dropped 89.2 percent over 34.2 months and the depression lasted 43 months, from August 1929 to March 1933. These results show the wisdom of the second theorem, which states: "There is no known method of forecasting the extent or duration of a primary movement."

Jack Schannep's Not-So-Famous Editorial

Not so famous but equally timely was my follow-up "editorial," which was written 70 years later and posted in the Subscriber's Area of my web site (www.thedowtheory.com). In this article, I point out the similarities with Hamilton's famous editorial, confirm the then recent Dow Theory sell signal, and point out the uncanny parallels between the two then existing U.S. Presidents. Indeed, 1929 and 1999 did have a lot in common.

A Turn in the Tide—Part II

On October 25th, 1929, William Hamilton, Editor of the *Wall Street Journal*, and the successor to Charles Dow, wrote in his most famous editorial "A Turn in the Tide," that (two days earlier) the Dow Theory "gave the signal for a bear market in stocks." He noted that "There are people trading in Wall Street, and many all over the country, who have never seen a real bear market. . . . What is more material is that the stock market does forecast the general business of the country. The big bull market was confirmed by six years of prosperity and if the stock market takes the other direction there will be a contraction in business later. . . . " Of course he did not expect the stock market to drop 86% from that point and business to enter a great depression, but both happened. The Dow Theory does not predict the duration nor extent of such changes, only that change is coming.

In 1999, when the Dow Jones Industrial Average dropped below 10,466.93, the Dow Theory "gave the signal for a bear market in stocks." Certainly "there are people trading in Wall Street, and many all over the country, who have never seen a real bear market," in fact we have been in bull markets for 97% of the time over the last 17 years. And the rest of his quote is also correct: 82% of all bear markets in the 20th Century have been followed by "a contraction in business later" whether it be an official recession, or just a "mild" or "growth" one, or "really big one" like the depression. Fortunately, most "real bear markets," which I define as a drop of at least 16% on both the Dow Jones Industrials *and* the Standard & Poor's 500 Index, are not as severe as the 1929–32 experience. They average a not insignificant −34% drop over an 18-month time frame. The "traditional" definition of a 20% drop is widely used but unfortunately excludes several "real" bear markets and their following recessions such as 1923, 1956–57, and 1978–80. Whichever definition you use, a Dow Theory "Sell" signal has been followed by bear markets more times than not.

I won't dwell on the many similarities of the 1929 stock market and that of 1999, such as the record high price to earnings ratio, the price to book value, low dividend yields, etc., etc. But one uncanny parallel you may not be aware of is the almost identical headlines out of Washington, D.C., then and now:

In 1929, from the Chicago Tribune Press Service:

Washington, D.C., June 1—(Special)—Rapid retirement of the public debt will continue to be an administration policy under President Hoover and Secretary of the Treasury Mellon. Despite a program for increased expenditures for public works and a possibility of another tax cut within a year or two, it is estimated that the outstanding public debt can be substantially wiped out within less than 18 years. Retirements through the sinking fund . . . **will pay off the entire debt**, now standing at a little less than $17,000,000,000, **by 1947**. By adding to these debt retirements surplus revenues the debt can be paid off in a somewhat shorter period.

As for 1999, from www.whitehouse.gov came the following on February 17th: "Today, President Clinton will hold an event at the White House to discuss the importance of saving the majority of our future budget surpluses to ensure the long-term solvency of Social Security and Medicare and pay down the national debt, helping reduce the future burden on young people and grow the economy for years to come. . . . By practicing fiscal responsibility, the Administration's proposal will pay down nearly $3 trillion ($3,000,000,000,000) of our national debt. . . . President Clinton's proposal would cut the debt held by the public, as a share of the economy, to 7.1 percent in 2014. This would mean that instead of leaving a mountain of debt for our children, we would **completely eliminate the national debt by 2018**." Shortly after the publication of this press release, President Clinton updated the above on September 27th. He said, "*We can do all that and still have an affordable tax cut for the middle class and pay down our debt so that by 2015 we are debt-free for the first time since 1835, when Andrew Jackson was President.*"

The more things change, the more they stay the same. I wouldn't expect 1999 to parallel 1929 exactly, only that the tide of the stock market had changed once again. We shall see.

Written and posted September 1999 on the Schannep Timing Indicator & TheDowTheory.com web site

Author's note: I have added italics and bold to emphasize particular points. There was a bear market from January–March 2000 to September 2001 in which nearly 1 in 10 stocks lost 90 percent in value. The final low after the 2000 highs was 33 months later, in October 2002, for a total loss by the Dow Jones Industrial Average of nearly 38 percent, "somewhat" less than in 1929 to 1932 but almost the exact same 34-month time frame. As for the plans of Presidents Hoover and Clinton for eliminating the national debt, both were swept up in the optimism prevailing at the time. Hoover's plan was done in by the Depression; Clinton's, by 9/11 and the ensuing costs of the war on terrorism.

Now that we have some history and the "rules" firmly in place and have seen how they worked in 1929 and 1999, let's look into the specifics of the signals for their use now and into the future.

Signals Described

N ow that we have a thorough understanding of the hypothesis and theorems used for interpreting the Dow Theory, we will begin to focus on the price patterns on the Dow Jones Industrials and the Transportation Average that constitute Dow Theory buy and sell signals. In this chapter, we discuss the classic patterns of Dow Theory buy and sell signals and some of the more typical variations for each. Interestingly, you will see that the patterns are similar but inverted for buys and sells. These patterns develop at the rate of about one per year, sometimes more often (with bear markets) and sometimes less often (with bull markets). I can assure you they will continue to develop in the future, and I think we can assume they will be just as profitable in the future as they have been in the past.

Identifying Patterns of Change from a Bull Market to a Bear and Vice Versa

During the primary trend of bull markets, there are pullbacks (secondary reactions) of *usually* 5 to 15 percent for both the Industrial Average and the Transportation Average. After a pullback, there is a bounce that *must exceed 3 percent on either one* of the averages to be meaningful from a Dow Theory standpoint. According to Robert Rhea, in a bear market, the secondary reaction takes the form of a bounce and then the pullback must be 3 percent. *That is really the only hard-and-fast number in the Dow Theory.*

While neither the primary nor the secondary trends have been specifically defined, my own research shows that a bull market primary trend will have advanced in excess of 19 percent on both the Dow Jones and Standard & Poor's 500 indices. A bear market primary trend will have declined in excess of 16 percent on both. A review of the Dow Theory signals shows that a secondary trend will usually bounce at least 4 percent on both the Industrials and Transportation indices, and usually one or both will exceed 7 percent.

According to *The Dow Theory*, Robert Rhea writes that secondary reactions "*usually* last from three *weeks* to as many *months*, during which . . . the price movement *generally* retraces from 33 per cent to 66 per cent of the primary price change." But in the same book, Dow's successor, William Peter Hamilton, described "secondary reactions . . . [as] lasting from a few *days* to many *weeks*."

While the *duration* of secondary reactions is not absolutely precise, what is precisely defined is the *extent* of the return move. After a bull market top, following a secondary reaction pullback there will be a bounce. This bounce must exceed 3 percent on either of the averages to become part of a Dow Theory signal. Conversely, the bounce up from a bear market bottom will be followed by a pullback, which must exceed 3 percent on either of the averages to become part of a Dow Theory signal. That means that the secondary reaction must drop in a bull market or rise in a bear market enough that the next return move can exceed 3 percent without necessarily violating the prior bull market top or the prior bear market low. The next examples should give you a better idea of how this works out in forming or aborting a signal.

Bull Market Buy Signals

The classic buy signal is developed in this way: After the low point of a primary downtrend in a bear market is established, a secondary uptrend bounce will occur. After that, a pullback on one of the averages must exceed 3 percent and must then, ideally, hold above the prior lows on both the Industrial and the Transportation Averages. Finally, a breakout above the previous rally high by both constitutes a buy signal for the developing bull market.

The classic buy (B-1) can be outlined in this way:

1. Market lows.
2. Bounce.
3. Pullback (hold above the lows).
4. Break up (above the bounce high).

Figure 2.1 represents how the Dow Jones Industrial Average and the Transportation Average might look. The patterns on this and the following charts shown for each Average are interchangeable; that is to say, the Industrial could follow the course shown for the Transports, and vice versa. Examples can be found in Appendix A, where you will find B-1 type signals in 1922, 1933, and so on, and most recently in 2003.

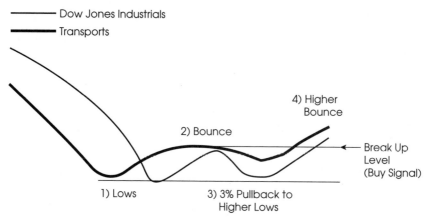

Figure 2.1   Classic Buy Signal (B-1)

More than one bounce can occur within the confines of the bounce highs and the lows. Any such nonconfirmation by the other average is inconsequential.

There are at least four acceptable variations of the pattern.

Buy (B-2) (see Figure 2.2)

1. Market lows.
2. Bounce.
3. Pullback (one index makes a new low).
4. Break up.

Appendix A presents B-2 type signals in 1923, 1943, and 1970.

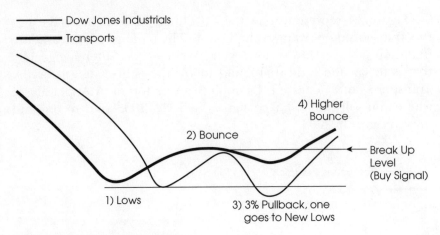

Figure 2.2   Buy Signal (B-2)

Buy (B-3) (see Figure 2.3)

1. Market lows.
2. Bounce.
3. Pullback.
4. Break up (one only).
5. Pullback (other makes lower low).
6. Break up (over both bounce highs).

Appendix A presents B-3 type signals in 1961 and 1967.

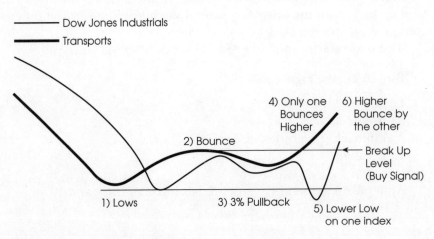

Figure 2.3   Buy Signal (B-3)

Buy (B-4) (see Figure 2.4)

1. Market low.
2. Bounce.
3. Pullback (one may go to new low).
4. Lower bounce (on one or both).
5. Lower pullback (another new low).
6. Break up (over first bounces)

Appendix A presents a B-4 type signal in 1988.

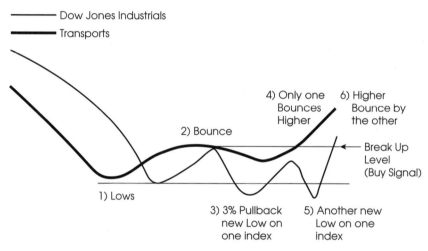

Figure 2.4   Buy Signal (B-4)

Buy (B-5)

1. Market low.
2. Bounce.
3. Pullback on one only.
4. New all-time highs on both.

Appendix A presents a B-5 type signal in 1954, when the transports exceeded their previous all-time high.

Other combinations of these signals can occur with nonconfirmations (divergences) at various points and still qualify as signals. New all-time highs negate the need for pullbacks to confirm a new buy.

Bear Market Sell Signals

A bear market sell signal is determined in much the same way that buy signals are, but opposite to a buy signal. When a bull market tops and has a secondary reaction setback, and the subsequent rally that goes back up (again, over 3 percent) falls short of reaching the previous high and then penetrates the recent lows on the next decline as measured by both the Industrial and Transportation Averages, a sell signal is generated indicating a bear market.

The classic sell (S-1) can be outlined as:

1. Market highs.
2. Pullback.
3. Bounce (to below the highs).
4. Break down (below pullback).

(See Figure 2.5.)
Appendix A presents S-1 type signals in 1921, 1929, and so on, and most recently in 2002.

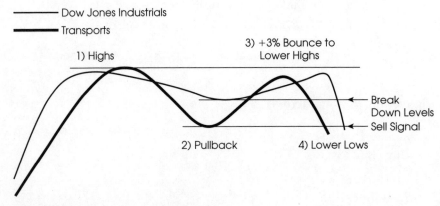

Figure 2.5   Classic Sell Signal (S-1)

There are at least two other acceptable variations of the pattern.

Sell (S-2) (see Figure 2.6)

1. Market highs.
2. Pullback.
3. Bounce (one makes a new high).
4. Break down.

Examples can be found in Appendix A, where you will find S-2 type signals in 1923, 1960, and so on, and most recently in 2003.

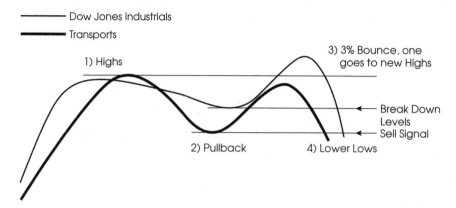

Figure 2.6   Sell Signal (S-2)

Sell (S-3) (see Figure 2.7)

1. Market highs.
2. Pullback.
3. Bounce (one makes a new high)
4. Pullback (other makes a new low)
5. Bounce (first makes a newer high)
6. Break down (below both pullback)

Examples can be found in Appendix A, where you will find S-2 type signals in 1923, 1943, and 1970.

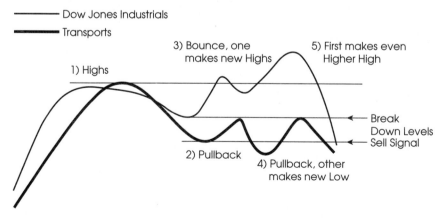

Figure 2.7   Sell Signal (S-3)

I have included descriptions and illustrations of both bear sell signals and bull buy signals to demonstrate that most buy and sell signals will fit into one or the other of these patterns. Moreover, in Appendix A, I have identified the types of signals so that investors may be better able to identify such signals in the future. These Dow buy and sell signals are important indicators for investors to know and understand.

CHAPTER 3

A Look at the Record

The complete record of the Dow Theory's results have been difficult to come by until I compiled the "Official" Complete and Detailed Record of the Original Dow Theory shown in Appendix A. These results have been formulated from various sources, including contacts with a number of experts, from articles in various journals and books, and from my own interpretation. Specifically, *Technical Analysis of Stock Trends* by Robert D. Edwards, John Magee, and W. H. C. Bassetti, which is generally considered the "bible" of technical analysis, was invaluable in determining early twentieth-century signals. Originally published in 1948, it is now in its ninth edition. Recent editions have incorporated my interpretation of the Dow Theory to bring its record up to date from 1956 into the twenty-first century. In this chapter, I reprint material from the eighth edition. Then I discuss the results. I think you'll find their way of presenting the results and the financial results of utilizing the Dow Theory interesting.

The Dow Theory in the Twentieth and Twenty-First Centuries

Next we turn to portions of *Technical Analysis of Stock Trends*. In the next section, I discuss the implications of this record.

Technical Analysis of Stock Trends*

As may be seen in the following table [Table 3.1], the Dow Theory continued to provide its user an advantage over the unaware investor. From its original investment of $100 in 1897 the investment would have grown to $362,212.97 by the end of the 20th century. The Editor initiated the update of the previous data in October 1956 with capital of $11,236.65 garnered from the trades described in Chapter 5. To my mind this table is an astounding demonstration of the power of methodical technical investing.

By contrast, the investment of $100, if bought at the low, 29.64, and sold at the all-time high, 11762.71, in January 2000 (up to the publication of this Edition) would have grown to $39,685.03. It makes one wonder whether those chaps running around predicting a Dow of 36000 are so crazy after all.

Here the record continues made by a different hand. [See Table 3.2.] I am indebted to Jack Schannep of TheDowTheory .com (www.thedowtheory.com) for the data recapitulated here. At that URL, a very enlightening exposition of the Theory and its record may be found—much more complete than that which is found here.

Minor discrepancies are noted within these and others' data, a point which will be raised by purists. This is occasioned by disagreements within the priestly circles of those who keep the sacred records. That is, not all theorists are in 100% agreement as to the exact date or nature of the signals. (Some will say the reentry date of October 1, 1956, should have been October 7, 1957, for example.) Meaning, of course, that some judgment is involved in interpretation of the entrails. The Dow Theory is not an objective algorithm, just as chart analysis is not reducible to an objective algorithm. (I am allowed to jest at the priesthood as I am a junior acolyte in these matters. It would not be seemly for the uninitiated to burlesque.)"

In brief, an investment of $100 in 1897 would have become $11,236.65 in 1956 simply by buying the Industrial Average

---

*Copyright 2001 from *Technical Analysis of Stock Trends*, 8th edition (pages 49–51), by Robert D. Edwards, John Magee, and W.H.C. Bassetti. Reproduced by permission of Routledge/Taylor & Francis Group, LLC, New York.

Table 3.1 Dow Theory's 103-Year Record

Original Fund $100	Date	Industrial Average Price	% Gain	Proceeds
Invested	July 12, 1897	44.61		
Stocks sold	December 16, 1899	63.84	43.1	$143.10
Proceeds reinvested	October 20, 1900	59.44		
Stocks sold	June 1, 1903	59.59	0.3	143.53
Proceeds reinvested	July 12, 1904	51.37		
Stocks sold	April 26, 1906	92.44	80.0	258.35
Proceeds reinvested	April 24, 1908	70.01		
Stocks sold	May 3, 1910	84.72	21.0	312.60
Proceeds reinvested	October 10, 1910	81.91		
Stocks sold	January 14, 1913	84.96	3.7	324.17
Proceeds reinvested	April 9, 1915	65.02		
Stocks sold	August 28, 1917	86.12	32.5	429.53
Proceeds reinvested	May 13, 1918	82.16		
Stocks sold	February 3, 1920	99.96	21.7	522.74
Proceeds reinvested	February 6, 1922	83.70		
Stocks sold	June 20, 1923	90.81	8.5	567.17
Proceeds reinvested	December 7, 1923	93.80		
Stocks sold	October 23, 1929	305.85	226.1	1849.54
Proceeds reinvested	May 24, 1933	84.29		
Stocks sold	September 7, 1937	164.39	95.0	3606.61
Proceeds reinvested	June 23, 1938	127.41		
Stocks sold	March 31, 1939	136.42	7.2	3866.29
(Corrected Figures:		131.84	3.5	3732.28)
Proceeds reinvested	July 17, 1939	142.58		
Stocks sold	May 13, 1940	137.50	(Loss 3.6)	3727.10
Proceeds reinvested	February 1, 1943	125.88		
Stocks sold	August 27, 1946	191.04	51.9	5653.71
Proceeds reinvested	October 2, 1950	228.94		
Stocks sold	April 2, 1953	280.03	22.3	6911.01
Proceeds reinvested	January 19, 1954	288.27		
Stocks sold	October 1, 1956	468.70	62.6	11,236.65

stocks each time the Dow Theory announced a Bull Market and holding them until the Dow Theory announced a Bear Market. During this period, the investor would have made 15 purchases and 15 sales, or about one transaction every 2 years on average.

Taking this $11,236.65 in 1956 and continuing to buy and sell on Dow Theory signals, the technical investor would have

Table 3.2   Dow Theory's 103-Year Record Continued

Original Fund $100	Date	Industrial Average Price	% Gain	Proceeds
Proceeds reinvested	January 19, 1954	288.27		$6911.01
Stocks sold	October 1, 1956	468.70	62.59	$11,236.65
Proceeds reinvested	May 2, 1958	459.56		$11,236.65
Stocks sold	March 3, 1960	612.05	33.18	$14,965.17
Proceeds reinvested	October 10, 1961	706.67		$14,965.17
Stocks sold	April 26, 1962	678.68	−3.96	$14,372.43
Proceeds reinvested	November 9, 1962	616.13		$14,372.43
Stocks sold	May 5, 1966	899.77	46.04	$20,988.88
Proceeds reinvested	January 11, 1967	822.49		$20,988.88
Stocks sold	October 24, 1967	888.18	7.99	$22,665.20
Proceeds reinvested	October 1, 1968	942.32		$22,665.20
Stocks sold	February 25, 1969	899.80	−4.51	$21,642.49
Proceeds reinvested	October 27, 1969	860.28		$21,642.49
Stocks sold	January 26, 1970	768.88	−10.62	$19,343.09
Proceeds reinvested	September 28, 1970	758.97		$19,343.09
Stocks sold	July 28, 1971	872.01	14.89	$22,224.03
Proceeds reinvested	February 10, 1972	921.28		$22,224.03
Stocks sold	March 23, 1973	922.71	0.16	$22,258.52
Proceeds reinvested	November 5, 1974	674.75		$22,258.52
Stocks sold	October 24, 1977	802.32	18.91	$26,466.78
Proceeds reinvested	June 6, 1978	866.51		$26,466.78
Stocks sold	October 19, 1978	846.41	−2.32	$25,852.84
Proceeds reinvested	May 13, 1980	816.89		$25,852.84
Stocks sold	July 2, 1981	959.19	17.42	$30,356.34
Proceeds reinvested	October 7, 1982	965.97		$30,356.34
Stocks sold	January 25, 1984	1231.89	27.53	$38,713.07
Proceeds reinvested	January 21, 1985	1261.37		$38,713.07
Stocks sold	October 15, 1987	2355.09	86.71	$72,280.75
Proceeds reinvested	January 7, 1988	2051.89		$72,280.75
Stocks sold	October 13, 1989	2569.26	25.21	$90,505.85
Proceeds reinvested	June 4, 1990	2935.19		$90,505.85
Stocks sold	August 3, 1990	2809.65	−4.28	$86,634.86
Proceeds reinvested	December 5, 1990	2610.40		$86,634.86
Stocks sold	August 4, 1998	8487.31	225.13	$281,679.77
Proceeds reinvested	September 15, 1998	8024.39		281,679.77
Stocks sold	September 23, 1999	10318.59	28.59	$362,212.97

had $362,212.97 in pocket when he sold at the end of the 20th century as opposed to the $39,685.03 of his dozing counterpart, or the Trust Department of the Rip Van Winkle Bank of Sleepy Hollow. And, in addition, he would not have been deliquidified during Bear Markets.

Whether or not the Dow Theory retains its mojo over the market as a whole, there can be no question that it still calls the turn for its sector of the market, which as Jack Schannep correctly notes, has five times the capitalization of the NASDAQ.

A Look at the Results

Appendix A presents the complete and detailed record of the traditional Dow Theory showing the makeup of the various signals and their signal type, and their market levels in relation to subsequent bull and bear market levels.

Figure 3.1 presents a graphic representation of the Dow Theory record. The white sections represent the periods following buy signals. The black represent periods following sell signals. Each phase is assumed to continue until there is an offsetting signal. As you can see, buy signals capture most of the bull market's advances, and sell signals generally avoid most of the bear market's declines.

So how does it work out in the stock market? Table 3.3 shows the results for the Standard & Poor's (S&P) 500 three months, six months, nine months, and a year after the Dow Theory buy signals with the average gains being +5.1 percent, +11.6 percent, +14.3 percent, and +19.5 percent respectively, dividents not included. The average annual gain from buy to sell was 18.7 percent including dividends.

Sells do not have the downside potential (the stock market can't really go to zero) that buys have to the upside (unlimited), and historically bear markets have lasted only half as long as bull markets. Table 3.4 presents the results after sells showing the further downside to the market lows. The average further loss is –12.8 percent over the next 5.8 months.

Author's note: When no official bear market follows, an asterisk marks the low for this move. Twelve signals were followed by official bear markets, 10 were not.

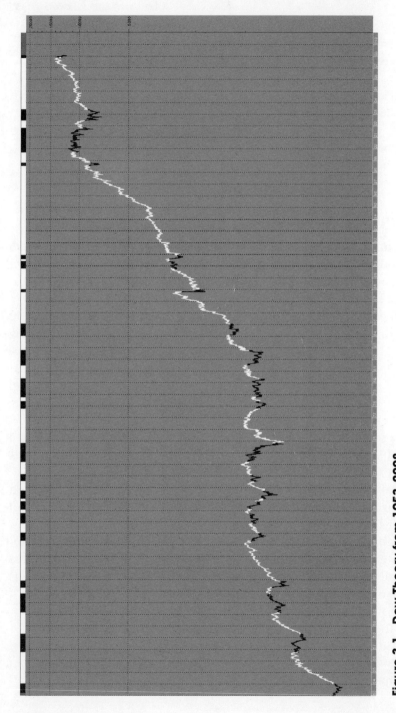

Figure 3.1   Dow Theory from 1953–2008

Table 3.3 Original Dow Theory Buy Signals and the S&P 500 Gain Thereafter

Date	Level	3 Months		6 Months		9 Months		1 Year		To Next Sell Signal		
		Level	% Gain	Level	% Gain	Level	% Gain	Level	% Gain	Date	Level	% Gain
1/19/1954	25.68	27.76	8.1	29.98	16.7	31.91	24.3	34.96	36.1	10/1/1956	44.70	74.1
5/2/1958	43.69	47.49	8.7	51.33	17.5	55.21	26.4	57.65	32.0	3/3/1960	54.78	25.4
10/10/1961	68.11	68.96	1.2	68.56	0.7	67.05*	−1.6			4/26/1962	67.05	−1.6
11/9/1962	58.78	66.17	12.6	70.35	19.7	70.48	19.9	73.36	24.8	5/5/1966	87.53	48.9
1/11/1967	83.47	88.88	6.5	92.48	10.8	96.37	15.5	94.42*	13.1	10/24/1967	94.42	13.1
10/1/1968	102.9	103.86	1.0	97.98*	−4.7					2/25/1969	97.98	−4.74
10/27/1969	97.94	88.17*	−10.0							1/26/1970	88.17	−10.0
9/28/1970	83.86	91.09	8.6	99.95	19.2	97.74	16.6	97.07	15.7	7/28/1971	97.07	15.8
2/10/1972	105.6	105.42	−0.2	111.05*	5.2	113.73	7.7	114.68	8.6	3/23/1973	108.88	3.1
11/5/1974	75.11	78.95	5.1	90.08	19.9	86.23	14.8	89.15	18.7	10/24/1977	91.63	22.0
6/6/1978	100.3	105.38	5.0	99.33*	−1.0					10/19/1978	99.33	−1.0
5/13/1980	106.3	123.28	16.0	136.49	28.4	126.98	19.5	130.55	22.8	7/2/1981	128.64	21.0
10/7/1982	128.8	145.18	12.7	151.76	17.8	167.56	30.1	170.8	32.6	1/25/1984	164.84	28.0
1/21/1985	175.2	181.11	3.4	195.13	11.4	186.96	6.7	205.79	17.4	10/15/1987	298.08	70.1
1/7/1988	261.1	266.16	0.2	271.78	4.1	278.07	6.5	280.67	7.5	10/13/1989	333.62	27.8
6/4/1990	367.4	344.86*	−6.1							8/3/1990	344.86	−6.1
12/5/1990	329.9	376.72	14.2	385.09	16.7	389.14	18.3	377.39	14.4	8/4/1998	1072.1	225.0
11/2/1998	1111.6	1262.0	13.5	1335.18	20.1	1328.05	19.5	1280.4	15.1	9/23/1999	1280.41	15.2
11/8/2001	1119	1096.2	−2.0	1088.85	−2.7	976.14*	−12.7			6/25/2002	976.14	−12.7
6/4/2003	986.24	1027.9	4.2	1069.72	8.5	1154.88	17.1	1122.55	13.8	11/21/07	1416.77	43.7
Average % Gain:			5.1		11.6		14.3		19.5			29.9

*Ends at a Dow Theory sell signal during this 3-month period.

Table 3.4   Dow Theory Sell Signals and the Further S&P 500 Loss to the Final Bear Market Lows

Sell Date	Level	Low Date	Level	Loss after Sell	Months to Low
4/2/1953	25.23	9/14/1953	22.71*	10.0%	5.4
10/1/1956	44.70	10/22/1957	38.98	12.8%	12.7
3/3/1960	54.78	10/25/1960	52.30*	4.5%	7.7
4/26/1962	67.05	6/26/1962	52.32	22.0%	2.0
5/5/1966	87.53	10/7/1966	73.20	16.4%	5.1
10/24/1967	94.42	3/5/1968	87.72*	7.1%	4.4
2/25/1969	97.98	7/29/1969	89.48*	8.7%	5.1
1/26/1970	88.17	5/26/1970	69.29	21.4%	4.0
7/28/1971	97.07	11/23/1971	90.16*	7.1%	3.8
3/23/1973	108.88	8/22/1973	100.53*	7.7%	5.0
10/24/1977	91.63	3/6/1978	86.90	5.2%	4.4
10/19/1978	99.33	11/14/1978	92.49	6.9%	0.8
7/2/1981	128.64	8/12/1982	102.42*	20.4%	13.3
1/25/1984	164.84	7/24/1984	147.82*	10.3%	6.1
10/15/1987	298.08	12/4/1987	223.92	24.9%	1.6
10/13/1989	333.62	1/30/1990	322.98*	3.2%	3.6
8/3/1990	344.86	10/11/1990	295.46	14.3%	2.3
8/4/1998	1072.12	8/31/1998	957.28	10.7%	0.9
9/23/1999	1280.41	9/21/2001	965.80	24.6%	23.0
6/25/2002	976.14	7/23/2002	797.70*	18.3%	0.9
11/21/2007	1416.77				
			Average	12.8%	5.6

*When no bear market follows this is the low for the move.

While no two Dow Theorists ever seem able to agree on each and every signal given, I believe that the record shown here and in Appendix A is as true and correct an interpretation of the Dow Theory as I can make. I have relied on the experts' consensus up until the mid-1960s, when they treated 1966 to 1974 as a single bear market. I see three bear markets that fit my definition (to be discussed in Chapter 6) in that time frame with two accompanying recessions and two bull markets (as defined in Chapter 5). Therefore, I have proceeded with a more sensible and responsive interpretation. I feel that the time parameters used by the theory when it was devised early in the twentieth century need to be updated to reflect the realities of the twenty-first century. Anyone who has read Alvin Toffler's *Third Wave* knows that things happen faster now than they did then. But I am getting ahead of myself;

Table 3.5   Dow Theory Sells and Following Bear Markets and Recessions

Dow Theory Sell Date	Bear Market Start (mo/yr)	Bear Market End (mo/yr)	Recession Start (mo/yr)	Recession End (mo/yr)
6/1/1903	none		9/02	8/04
4/26/1906	1/06	11/07	5/07	6/08
5/3/1910	11/09	9/11	1/10	1/12
1/14/1913	9/12	7/14	1/13	12/14
8/28/1917	11/16	12/17	8/18	3/19
2/3/1920	11/19	8/21	1/20	7/21
6/20/1923	3/23	10/23	5/23	7/24
none	none		10/26	11/27
10/23/1929	9/29	7/32	8/29	3/33
9/7/1937	3/37	3/38	5/37	6/38
3/31/1939	11/38	4/42	none	
5/13/1940	11/38	4/42	none	
none	none		2/45	10/45
8/27/1946	5/46	6/49	none	
11/9/1948	5/46	6/49	11/48	10/49
4/2/1953	none		7/53	5/54
10/1/1956	4/56	10/57	8/57	4/58
3/3/1960	none		4/60	2/61
4/26/1962	12/61	6/62	none/"mild"	
5/5/1966	2/66	10/66	none/"growth recession"*	
10/24/1967	none		none	
2/25/1969	12/68	5/70	12/69	11/70
1/26/1970	12/68	5/70	12/69	11/70
7/28/1971	none		none	
3/23/1973	1/73	12/74	11/73	3/75
10/24/1977	9/76	2/78	none	
10/19/1978	9/78	4/80	1/80	7/80
7/2/1981	4/81	8/82	7/81	11/82
1/25/1984	none		none/"soft landing"†	
10/15/1987	8/87	10/87	none	
10/13/1989	none		7/90	3/91
8/3/1990	7/90	10/90	7/90	3/91
8/4/1998	7/98	8/98	none	
9/23/1999	1/00	9/01	3/01	11/01
6/25/2002	3/02	10/02	none	
11/21/2008	10/07		12/07	

*Forbes, January 23, 1989.
†Wall Street Journal, October 11, 2000.

Table 3.6   Dow Theory Buys and Following Bull Markets and Economic Expansions

Dow Theory Buy Date	Bull Market (Dow Jones) Start (mo/yr)	Bull Market (Dow Jones) End (mo/yr)	Expansion Start (mo/yr)	Expansion End (mo/yr)
10/20/1900	9/00	6/01	12/00	9/02
7/12/1904	11/3	1/06	8/04	5/07
4/24/1908	11/07	11/09	6/8	1/10
10/10/1910	9/11	9/12	1/12	1/13
4/9/1915	7/14	11/16	12/14	8/18
5/13/1918	12/17	11/19	3/19	1/20
2/6/1922	8/21	3/23	7/21	5/23
12/7/1923	10/23	9/29	7/24	10/26
12/7/1923	10/23	9/29	11/27	8/29
5/24/1933	7/32	3/37	3/33	5/37
6/23/1938	3/38	11/38	6/38	2/45
7/17/1939	none		6/38	2/45
2/1/1943	4/42	5/46	6/38	2/45
2/1/1943	4/42	5/46	10/45	11/48
5/14/1948	6/49	4/56	10/49	7/53
10/2/1950	6/49	4/56	10/49	7/53
1/19/1954	6/49	4/56	5/54	8/57
5/2/1958	10/57	12/61	4/58	4/60
10/10/1961	6/62	2/66	2/61	12/69
11/9/1962	6/62	2/66	2/61	12/69
1/11/1967	10/66	12/68	2/61	12/69
10/1/1968	10/66	12/68	2/61	12/69
10/27/1969	5/70	1/73	11/70	11/73
9/28/1970	5/70	1/73	11/70	11/73
2/10/1972	5/70	1/73	11/70	11/73
11/5/1974	12/74	9/76	3/75	1/80
6/6/1978	2/78	9/78	3/75	1/80
5/13/1980	4/80	4/81	7/80	7/81
10/7/1982	8/82	8/87	11/82	7/90
1/21/1985	8/82	8/87	11/82	7/90
1/7/1988	10/87	7/90	11/82	7/90
6/4/1990	10/90	7/98	3/91	3/01
12/5/1990	10/90	7/98	3/91	3/01
9/15/1998	8/98	1/00	3/91	3/01
11/8/2001	9/01	3/02	11/01	12/07?
6/4/2003	10/02	10/07	11/01	12/07?

more on that in Chapter 8. An example of this more responsive interpretation was the buy signal on November 2, 1998, at 8,706 while other Dow Theory newsletters waited until after 11,000 was reached in May 1999 to recommend a buy! This point will be elaborated on in the next chapter.

In the Foreword to *The Dow Theory,* Hugh Bancroft states: "What has come to be spoken of as the Dow Theory is in effect the combined market wisdom of the late Charles H. Dow and William Peter Hamilton." It was Hamilton who "developed what he called the 'implications' of Dow's theory. To Hamilton the stock market was a **barometer of business**, a barometer which **also frequently forecast its own probable future trend.**" In 1922, he wrote *The Stock Market Barometer: A Study of Its Forecast Value Based on Charles H. Dow's Theory of the Price Movement.* It was reissued by John Wiley & Sons in 1998 as part of their Wiley Investment Classics series.

How well that theory has worked in forecasting bear markets and recessions/depressions is evident from Table 3.5.

The Dow Theory sell signals have been associated with *19* of the *21* recessions (and three soft landings/mild or growth recessions) and *all 23* bear markets since 1903.

Don't get the impression that the Dow Theory catches most recessions and all bear markets because it is under a sell signal most of the time. Actually it has been in a buy mode for 63 percent of the time since 1900. Forecasting "business" and its own "probable future trend" also includes business expansions and bull markets, and Table 3.6 shows what an excellent job it has done.

The Dow Theory buy signals have preceded/confirmed and/or reconfirmed all business expansions and bull markets during the twentieth century. Can there be any doubt that the theory will not do the same in the twenty-first century? Despite this excellent, but of course not perfect, past history and documented record, there still exists a good bit of give-and-take about the Dow Theory, as we shall soon see.

CHAPTER 4

Give-and-Take about the Theory

There have been many times when Dow theorists did not agree on signals. Probably the most dramatic periods were from 1966 to 1975 and again in 1999. In the 1977 *Barron's* article "How Now, Dow Jones?" John Boland pointed out that his four experts treated the sell on May 5, 1966, as *one long bear market* until their buy on January 27, 1975. I, and some others, disagree. I see *three* bear markets that fit my definition in that time frame with two accompanying *recessions* and *two bull markets*. Consequently, I identified five Dow Theory signals to buy and sell in that 8.5-year time period when others saw none. Those signals are shown in Appendix A. The review of the most recent "disagreement," in 1999, that follows is a most definitive example.

From Agreement to Disagreement

It is rare when nearly all followers of the Dow Theory are in agreement on a signal, but that did happen in the summer of 1998. The Dow Jones Transportation Average reached its highest point on April 16 at the 3686 level, and a month later the Industrial Average made a high on May 13 at 9211. Therefore, both "sticks" were set in the sand at those high water marks. Both averages then set back into June with the Transports dropping 11 percent to 3259 on June 2 and Industrials dropping 6 percent to 8627 on June 15. Everyone agreed that was a secondary reaction in the "primary" uptrending bull market, the definitions for bull markets being all over the ballpark, as you will see in Chapter 5. The next thing that happened was an 11 percent bounce for Transports to 3618 on July 14. That rally failed to reach its stick in the sand. Meanwhile the Industrials resumed their uptrend and exceeded their prior top by rising 8 percent to 9337 on July 17, thus moving its stick farther uphill. This divergence, between the action of the Transports failing to make new highs and the Industrials, which did make new highs, set up a possible sell scenario. While this was not the classic pattern of both averages failing to make new highs, it was one of the more usual variations. It was similar to the S-2 signal shown in Chapter 2.

With the flow of the tide possibly subsiding, you look to see if the pullback from the recent up-moves will fall lower than the first pullbacks. On July 29 the Transports closed at 3244, a breaking below its previous low, and then on August 4 the Industrials did the same by closing at 8487. I have not used decimals in this discussion in order to keep it simple, although they are an integral part of closing prices. Table 4.1 shows how that sell signal shaped up.

It is too bad that the sell could not have been signaled *during* the day, as the Dow dropped through the 8627 previous low, rather than at the end of the day, which was down −299 points at 8487, but the use of the day's *closing prices* is another hard-and-fast rule set by Robert Rhea.

Another quote by Rhea will set the stage for the interpretation of the Dow Theory after the market lows of 7539 on August 31, 1998: "Any thinking man will readily realize that if the Dow Theory were infallible, or if even one or two men could always interpret its implications correctly, there would probably soon be no speculation in stocks." And we know there *is* speculation in stocks!

So what happened to the consensus? During the lows of that August, there was a capitulation or fear-motivated dumping of stocks,

Table 4.1   Undisputed Sell Signal

Date	Industrials	%	Status	Date	Transports	%
5/13/98	9211.84		Market highs	4/16/98	3686.02	
6/15/98	8627.93	−6.3	Pullback	6/2/98	3259.30	−11.6
7/19/98	9337.97	+8.2	Bull high/bounce	7/14/98	3618.73	+11.0
8/4/98	8487.31		Break down/sell	7/29/98	3244.93	

such as occurs at or near important bottoms, that *is* recognizable and *is* measurable. Rhea had written about the phenomenon, though he never called it "capitulation." While I doubt that I was the only one to notice the capitulation, I was, as far as I know, the only one to observe the pattern developing that led to an early Buy signal by the Dow Theory. The Transportation Average made a low on September 4 at 2617. Over the next 8 and 4 days respectively, both the Industrials and Transports rallied 6 and 5 percent, to 8021 and 2749 respectively. Two days later, they had fallen back −5 percent and −4 percent, to 7616 and 2632 respectively.

So here we had both pulling back over the prescribed 3 percent minimum and holding above the bear market lows. Purists will ask: "What about Hamilton's 'usually lasting from three weeks to as many months, during which interval the price movement generally retraces from 33 per cent to 66 per cent of the primary price change'?" Well, Hamilton also said: "The secondary reaction or rally in a bull or bear market, with a duration of a few days to a month or more." Therefore, given the capitulation that had occurred and the criteria having been met, when the Industrials closed at 8024 on September 15, above their prior bounce high, as the Transports had done the day before at 2805, I wrote: "The Dow Theory has just reversed itself with a new BUY signal today." Table 4.2 shows how it looked as a typical type B-1 buy signal, as explained in Chapter 2.

You'll notice that the secondary reaction (bounce) lasted less than a week for the Transports and only slightly more than a week for the Industrials. That is the reason others paid it little notice, at their peril.

A more "classic" reading of the Dow Theory might have considered the first bounce to have lasted just over three weeks and carried to 8154 (up 8 percent) by the Industrials and 2904 (up 11 percent) by the Transports on September 23, just under three weeks. The

Table 4.2   "Aggressive" Dow Theory Buy Signal

Date	Industrials	%	Status	Date	Transports	%
8/31/98	7539.07		Bear market lows	9/4/98	2616.75	
9/8/98	8020.78	+6.4	Bounce	9/8/98	2749.30	+5.1
9/10/98	7615.54	−5.1	Pullback	9/10/98	2631.51	−4.3
9/15/98	**8024.39**		Break up/**BUY**	9/14/98	2805.14	

pullback by the Industrials to 7633 (down –6%) on October 1 held above the previous lows, but the Transports dropped on down to new lows of 2345 on October 8. That divergence, while worrisome, was resolved favorably when the Transports rose to 2955 on November 2. By then, however, the Industrials had passed through to a higher high on October 15 and were at 8706. Table 4.3 shows how the B-2 buy signal shown in Chapter 2 looked. This is the signal I show in Appendix A.

This time the Transports were the last to reach new highs. The buy signal was over 400 points higher than it might have been, but *both* the Transports and the Industrials must confirm the signal. It is hard not to see the movement as a buy signal, yet one Dow Theorist actually explained that at the September bounce highs, the Transports had *only retraced 29 percent* (not 33 percent, although the Industrials had retraced 34 percent) and were a *few days* short (two actually) of three weeks (the Industrials had "barely" met the three-week time *guideline*). This "classic" buy is a *second* way to look at the Dow Theory, and waiting for the Transports to end their then-current divergence and to make new highs and then confirm the Industrials is yet a *third* way. Table 4.4 shows what two other leading Dow Theorists waited for, a type B-5 buy signal.

Table 4.3   The "Almost Classic" Dow Theory Buy Signal

Date	Industrials	%	Status	Date	Transports	%
8/31/98	7539.07		Bear market lows	9/4/98	2616.75	
9/23/98	8154.41	+8.1	Bounce	9/23/98	2904.10	+11.0
10/1/98	7632.53	–6.4	Pullback/new low	10/8/98	2345.00	–19.3
10/15/98	8299.36		Break up	11/2/98	2954.85	
11/2/98	**8706.50**		BUY			

Table 4.4   Result of a "Rigid" Dow Theory Interpretation

Date	Industrials	Status	Date	Transports
7/17/98	9337.97	All-time market highs	4/16/98	3686.02
8/31/98	7539.07	Bear market lows	9/4/98	2616.75
11/23/98	9374.27	Break up to newer highs	5/3/99	3696.59
5/3/99	**11,014.70**	**BUY**		

I was not surprised that no other Dow Theorist joined me with my buy at the 8024 level, but I was amazed that some did not see the turn of the tide until *after* the *11,000 level* was reached. My distress at what their poor interpretation of the Dow Theory was doing prompted me to contact Dave Kansas, then editor at TheStreet.com, with the idea that we (he) should help set the record straight. As a consequence, he asked Aaron Task, a senior writer at the time, to look into the situation. Task then wrote the article that follows, which is reprinted here with permission by TheStreet.com.

Dow Theory: It's Alive! Alive! And Bullish?

Beginning with the concept that it's always nice to have one thing *less* to worry about, we bring you: the Bride of Dow Theory.

Don't worry, this isn't a horror story and it actually has a happy ending (at least for those long the market).

The Dow Theory, you'll recall, is one of those time-honored, traditional measures of looking at the market, which (basically) says any move in the **Dow Jones Industrial Average** must be "confirmed" by the **Dow Jones Transportation Average**. The theory has been broadcasting a bearish signal since Aug. 4, according to its best-known proponents, and that's something other pundits generally include in their litany of things "wrong" with the market.

But Jack Schannep, president of The Dow Theory Investment Timing Newsletter, says Dow theory turned bullish Sept. 15 and remains so today.

According to purists, both indices would have to close at new all-time highs to re-establish a bullish signal. The Dow Jones Industrial Average, of course, has accomplished the feat several times since Aug. 4—most recently today, when it jumped 1.6% to 10,339.51. Nearly a year later, the Dow transportation average has yet to revisit (much less surpass) its all-time high of 3686.02, set April 16. Today, the transports fell 1% to 3335.89. [Author's Note: see Figure 4.1.]

Schannep, however, argues there was a "capitulation" last August, culminating in that frightful session Aug. 31, when the Dow fell 512.61 to close at 7539.07. The next day, the index traded as low as 7400.29, only to mount a remarkable recovery and close up 288.36 to 7827.43. Save for a few, brief reversals, the index hasn't much looked back since.

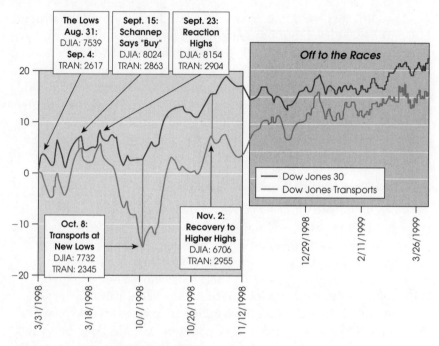

Figure 4.1 This Is a Bear Market?

The Dow transports made a low Sept. 4 at 2617. In days following their respective lows, the Dow industrials rose 6% while the transports gained 5%. They subsequently retraced 5% and 4% of those moves, respectively, but each held above its initial bear-market low. By Sept. 15, the industrials had bounced again to 8024, above their prior "bounce high," a feat the transports accomplished the day before when they hit 2805.

At that point, "Dow theory reversed itself with a new buy signal," Schannep says.

Relying on the Rule of Three

To make the call without either index hitting a new all-time high, the newsletter writer delved into some of the more esoteric aspects of Dow theory. Specifically, he referenced the so-called Rule of Three, first espoused by Robert Hamilton, who is credited with crystallizing Charles Dow's theory about the relationship between the industrial and transportation averages. Schannep also cites Robert Rhea, author of *The Dow Theory*.

The rule says a move of 3% or more by a major average is considered "significant." In the aftermath of the Aug. 31 lows, each average moved more than the requisite 3%, both in their respective bounces and subsequent reversals.

The second half of the Rule of Three says the reaction after a low (or high) will usually last from three weeks to three months and retrace from 33% to 66% of the "primary price change" from the prior high to the new low.

At this point, Schannep's view breaks from pure Dow theory. From their Aug. 31 closing low to the reaction high of 8154.41 on Sept. 23, the industrials retraced 34.2% of what had been lost from their July 17 high to the Aug. 1 low. But the transports only retraced 26.9% of what was lost between their April high and Sept. 4 low. Moreover, the time frame for the transports' "reaction" move fell two days short of the three-week guideline.

"We don't have the time frame, but even Hamilton said it could be only a matter of days," Schannep retorts. "Also, we exceed the 3% magic number. I will admit the buy signal was aggressive because we were in capitulation. But even if you weren't [in agreement then] you had to come up with a buy signal by now."

You Can't Do That

But the better-known Dow theorists have yet to embrace Schannep's interpretation or come around to his bullish way of thinking.

The man considered the dean of Dow theory, Richard Russell, editor and publisher of *Dow Theory Letters* in La Jolla, Calif., was downright dismissive of Schannep's call.

"It's not Dow theory. It's the Schannep theory," Russell says. "The next signal will be the bottom of a bear market. You don't get to a new bull market with the dividend yield at 1.6%. It's going to be a long-term bear market."

Chuck Carlson, contributing editor at *Dow Theory Forecasts* in Hammond, Ind., agrees Dow theory remains bearish but is a little more diplomatic.

"Hindsight obviously being 20-20, it's possible that [a buy] signal existed," Carlson says. "Our feeling is there wasn't enough of a retest in the transports once the market came off its bottom to warrant a change in the trend."

It's not clear there was a true "capitulation" during the late-August selloff, he adds, noting while the industrials never again traded below their Aug. 31 lows (to date), the transports "went back down to new lows" of 2345 on Oct. 8. "Our feeling was, the transports going to new lows didn't confirm the industrials and their ability to hold that low," he says.

Schannep concedes the transport average's slide to 2345 was "worrisome," but claims it was "resolved favorably" when the average subsequently recovered to 2954.85 on Nov. 2. By that time, he adds, the industrials were at 8706.15 after having established a "higher high"— above their Sept. 23 "reaction high"— of 8299.36 on Oct. 15.

Moreover, Schannep says his peers are being too doctrinaire in sticking to the 33% and three-week levels, noting they are "guidelines," not absolutes.

Adding he does not wish to get into a "shouting match" with his fellow Dow theorists, Schannep calls their clinging to a bearish stance "ludicrous."

"I'm just saying they're giving Dow theory a bum rap sticking to this interpretation," he says. "The world has got to know this is not a bear market up 33% from the lows. When they finally admit it, it's going to take the Dow transports at new highs, which is still a couple hundred points up. That means the Dow industrials will be between 10,000 and 11,000 after making a low at 7500."

Schannep may be a maverick. But looking at the performance of both averages, it seems he's a rebel *with* a clue.

By Aaron L. Task, Senior Writer
TheStreet.com
4/12/99 7:43 PM ET

Author's note: The other Dow Theorists actually issued buy signals at 11,014.69.

Other Views of the Dow Theory

In 1934, a Yale professor by the name of Alfred Cowles ran a test on the theory as espoused by Hamilton from his *Wall Street Journal* editorials over the period 1902 to 1929. His test "Can Stock Market Forecasters Forecast?" concluded that market timing based on the Dow Theory (as he surmised Hamilton to have utilized it) lagged a buy-and-hold strategy. His work was widely regarded as a landmark paper in the development of the "efficient market theory" made popular years later by Burton Malkiel, professor of economics at Princeton. Apparently Cowles used an asset mix of 50 percent Industrials and 50 percent Transports (due no doubt to the theory's use of both in determining its buy and sell signals). Cowles might better have used his market index, a value-weighted index of U.S. stocks that ultimately became the basis for the Standard & Poor's index. Cowles work was not risk adjusted; nonetheless, it placed chartists and Dow theorists in a very questionable position. Cowles saw *90* changes of position in the 27-year time frame. He was clearly not looking at the same Dow theory that I use if he had an average of 3.33 changes per year! There were seven bull and seven bear markets in those 27 years, so we might expect 14 or 15 signal changes, not six times that many.

It should be obvious that a market timer can prove his or her skill only by outperforming the market in down markets. (Using a market proxy like an index fund does not allow it to outperform in up markets.) Cowles's test ended with Hamilton's most famous sell signal on October 25, 1929, and so did not credit the Dow Theory with the 86 percent drop that followed. That call alone beat buy-and-hold for the next 25 years that it took the Dow Jones to regain the losses.

In 1998, two Yale professors named William Goetzmann and Alok Kumar, along with Stephen Brown from New York University, published "The Dow Theory: William Peter Hamilton's Track Record Re-Considered," wherein they reviewed Cowles's evidence and found that it *supports the contrary conclusion*: "that the Dow Theory . . . yielded positive risk-adjusted returns." They show that the "Hamilton portfolio was less volatile than the fully invested strategy" and outperformed the market from 1902 through 1927. I don't begin to understand "step-wise regression" and the "Artificial Intelligence Methods for Detecting Patterns" that they used, but it is obvious that neither did they follow the Dow Theory that I use. They found 3,599 buy calls, 1,143 sell calls, and 2,912 neutral calls. However, I will take their finding that "suggests a plain reason why the Dow Theory remains to this day a popular method for timing the market." According to Mark Hulbert, founder of *Hulbert Financial Digest* in Annandale, Virginia, the professors

> fed Hamilton's market-timing editorials from the early decades of the last century into neural networks, a type of artificial

intelligence software that can be 'trained' to detect patterns. Upon testing this neural network version of the Dow Theory over the nearly 70-year period from 1930 to the end of 1997, they found that it beat a buy-and-hold by an annual average of 4.4 percentage points per year.

In 1981, a couple of other academics, Rolf Wubbels of NYU and David Glickstein, an analyst with New York Life Insurance, wrote about their study in *Pensions & Investment Age* that "[p]redicting the market tides: Charles Dow's theory works" and that it stands "the test of time . . . surprisingly well."

In 1984, the longtime editor of *Barron's,* Robert N. Bleiberg, wrote a piece entitled "Way Above Average—For a Century Dow Theory Has Served Investors Well." He stated:

> [T]he venerable Dow Theory . . . boasts a long-term track record second to none. Over the years, it has regularly called major turns in the market, never at the top or bottom (the system precludes such pinpoint accuracy), but usually close enough to keep investors safely on the right side of the Street.

Criticisms and Comments

A typical comment about the Dow Theory is that it often does work but at times it does not. My answer would be: Did they read the assessment that the Theory is not infallible? It is, after all, rather naive to think that anything is infallible. Critics also point out that the imprecise definition of secondary reaction makes it difficult to be sure what the theory is saying and that, in fact, leading Dow Theorists often disagree on signals. Well, yes, the stock market and almost anything associated with it can be confusing. The definitions and examples of signals given in preceding chapters should help clarify the Theory. I am reminded of Robert Rhea's book, where it says:

> Any thinking man will readily realize that if the Dow Theory were infallible, or if even one or two men could always inter- pret its implications correctly, there would probably soon be no speculation in stocks.

It's almost like saying a little mystery makes it all the more intriguing. In this book, I've tried to remove some of the mystery, but I'm not sure I've dispelled all of it.

Some Wall Streeters suggest that the theory is late in giving its signals and misses the tops and bottoms by too wide a margin, as if to suggest that they have a method for doing better. This is, of course, one of the myths on Wall Street. No one sells at *the* top or buys at *the* bottom; can we all accept that? In fact, when Bernard Baruch, who spoke to my West Point class when I was a cadet, was asked how he made his fortune, he replied: "By never buying at the bottom or selling at the top." The Dow Theory assures that! Most professionals would agree that it is far better to buy *after* the bottom had been seen and to sell *after* the top. There again, the Dow Theory's very structure pretty well assures that its signals will be a bit late, but not *too* late to still be among the very best at market timing. From time to time, other "systems" will have better signals, but none has had better signals over the longer term.

The obvious criticism is that it doesn't predict the extent or duration of the market's movement—the bull or bear market! I'd also suggest that the theorem on primary movements states: "There is no known method of forecasting the extent or duration of a primary movement." Also: "The correct determination of the direction of this movement is the most important factor in successful speculation." Or as Dean Witter (now part of Morgan Stanley) publications have said over the years: "The genius of investing is recognizing the direction of a trend—not catching the highs or lows." And the Dow Theory does that.

Other criticisms have been repeated in light of the market at the end of the twentieth century and beginning of the twenty-first.

One criticism is that the Internet stocks and other high-tech stocks on the Nasdaq are where it is at and the Dow Theory seems to be pertinent only to the New York Stock Exchange (NYSE). W. H. C. (Charles) Bassetti (www.edwards-magee.com), editor and coauthor of the eighth edition of Edwards and Magee's *Technical Analysis of Stock Trends,* states that "there can be no question that it (the Dow Theory) still calls the turn for its sector of the market." The authors continue: "which[,] Jack Schannep correctly notes, has five times the capitalization of the NASDAQ." Notwithstanding my answer, Bassetti earlier had stated: "I now believe that only a composite of the three indexes (Dow Jones, Standard & Poors 500, and NASDAQ) can express the true state of the markets as a whole." He was referring to the need for such a composite to be in "harmonic convergence," which would eliminate the need for the Dow Jones Transports in the Dow Theory. Actually, there *are* many good reasons to use the Standard & Poor's (S&P) 500, but no good reasons to eliminate the Transports as I will discuss below. Another author also suggests the elimination of the Transports, and goes so far as to also eliminate the Industrials.

Pedro V. Marcel, in his *Market Timing with Technical Analysis,* uses the Nasdaq composite (COMP) in place of the Dow Jones Industrials (DJI) and the Amex Interactive Internet New Index (IIX) rather than the Transportation Averages (DJTA). He concludes:

> [W]e can postulate an extension of the Dow Theory as "The SPX" (Standard & Poor's 500) and COMP (Nasdaq) indices can be sub-stituted for the DJIA in the Dow theory. Similarly, the IIX and/ or the DOT (TheStreet.com Internet index) can be substituted for the DJTA in the Dow theory.

Maybe so, but I'll leave that to others. It is, of course, true that the hypotheses and theorems of the Dow Theory apply universally, but I'll settle for its relevance for the U.S. *major markets* and leave other areas alone.

One last observation regarding the Nasdaq before moving on. Traditionally, stocks have started trading over the counter (OTC) before moving up to the NYSE. Microsoft and Intel were two nota-ble exceptions for reasons known only to themselves. Even as the Nasdaq soared in the 1990s, the annual number of companies listed there started declining in 1996. On the NYSE, the number of list-ings rose to a five-year peak in 1999. Every year companies move up to the NYSE, and very rarely do any voluntarily move back to the Nasdaq. The debacle in 2000–2001 hardly seems likely to reverse that pattern. In that bear market, nearly 1 out of every 10 stocks in the Wilshire 5000 fell 90 percent or more, and *none* was in the Dow Jones Industrial Average. At least one and perhaps a few more were in the S&P 500, but the bulk of them were dot-com and other new or untested companies residing in the Nasdaq.

Another criticism refers to the fact that the Transportation Index is attacked at times as being irrelevant in the twenty-first century and given too much weight in the Dow Theory. Dow and Hamilton insisted that confirmation of a move by the Industrials be accompanied by the Transport, because "they always *did* confirm if the movement later proved to be genuine." The Transports (previously "Rails" but updated periodically to stay abreast of our changing times) supply industry with raw material, transport parts for assembly, and finally distribute finished products to consumers. This process goes hand in hand with the fortunes, or misfortunes, of the Industrial companies, so you would expect that their companies' stock movements would be aligned if a trend is to be believed. Actually, the Transportation Average is composed of 20 companies from five somewhat related industries: airlines, air freight, railroads, transport miscellaneous (including sea carriers), and trucking. When you look at America's 100 largest companies based on revenues—a list led by Wal-Mart, Exxon Mobil, General Motors, Ford, General Electric, ChevronTexaco, ConocoPhillips, Citigroup, American International, IBM, Hewlett-Packard, and the like—you are looking at companies that depend on transportation companies to distribute their products. Yes, the information age is using the mail (trucking and airlines), phones, faxes, the Internet, and other electronic means to gather and distribute services, but even that relies on the likes of FedEx and UPS, both companies in the Transportation Index.

You would think that some index more modern than the Transports could be found for use in the Dow Theory, but I am hard pressed to find anything that works as well. I have seen the highly successful results of the Dow Theory during the nineteenth and twentieth centuries using the Transportation Average for confirmation. The eighth edition of *Technical Analysis of Stock Trends* calculated that $100 in 1897 would have grown to nearly $15,000 in 1960 and then to over $362,000 by the year 2000 following the Dow Theory by buying and selling the Dow Jones Index. By contrast, buying with that $100 at *the very lowest point* of 29.64 and holding until the *very highest point* at 11,762.71 (at time of publication) would only have grown to $39,685! My own calculations show that equal amounts invested in 1960 would have almost exactly *doubled* in the Dow Theory as opposed to a buy and hold strategy. So, I say ignore the Transports and the Dow Theory at your own risk.

Even Dow Theorists themselves harbor misconceptions. In response to the criticism that the Theory gives late signals, they often respond that it is not necessary to wait for a signal to be completed, implying that you can proceed to beat the signal to the punch. I'm sorry, but that is not part of the Dow Theory. A signal is not complete until it is totally complete; anything short of that is anticipatory. There may be times when jumping the gun works (we shall discuss this under capitulation in Chapter 8), but from the standpoint of the original Dow Theory, proceeding without a signal is simply speculation.

A final misinterpretation has to do with "values." Numerous references are made to "value" by Hamilton as quoted in Rhea's book, but there is precious little explanation of what constitutes such "value." The word certainly is used often, but where is it written that a buy can occur *only* when *real values* are present? And who is to define what price to earnings ratio, yield, book value, and so on, qualifies as value? Charles Dow has been quoted as saying:

> It is always safer to assume that **values** determine prices in the long run. **Values** have nothing to do with current fluctuations. A worthless stock can go up five points just as easily as the best, but as a result of continuous fluctuations, the good stock will gradually work up to its investment **value**. [Bold added for emphasis.]

We all know it is better to buy stocks when they are obviously cheap and sell them when they are obviously dear, but the Dow Theory has no such requirement in its makeup. By its structure, it *may* give a buy signal when stocks are cheap*er* than previously and a sell signal when they are dear*er* than before, but that is by no means guaranteed. I say let the Dow Theory speak for itself and follow its signals whenever they may occur. Do not let personal preferences interfere. As Rhea's book put it: "The wish must never be allowed to father the thought."

Now that we have addressed some of the criticisms that have been voiced about the Dow Theory, we move into the interesting world of bull and bear markets.

PART II

BULLS AND BEARS

CHAPTER 5

Bull Markets

The Dow Theory presupposes that the stock market moves in persistent bull and bear trends. The "broad swing upward or downward" is, of course, the *major* trend (i.e., bull markets and bear markets) "extending from a year to three years." These are generalities, and unfortunately Wall Street, all these years later, still does not have *an explicit definition* of either bull or bear. A 20 percent advance or decline has come to be generally accepted as defining a bull or bear market, but I submit that while 20 percent is a *round* number, it is *not* the *right* number. My own studies show the appropriate figure for bull markets is a 19 percent advance and for bear markets, a 16 percent decline, as the information in this chapter explains.

Bull Markets in the Twentieth and Twenty-First Centuries

"Stocks tend to fluctuate" is a famous quote by J. P. Morgan from the 1930s, and it is a truism. The stock market goes up (a bull market) and down (a bear market). But beyond that, Wall Street, quite unbelievably, has no universally accepted definition of either. Bull markets have been defined as:

A **+13 percent** rise after 155 days or a **+30 percent** gain after 50 days — Ned Davis Research

A **+20 percent** rise — *Wall Street Journal*

A period in which stocks rise by **+300 percent**
   or more without being interrupted by a
   correction of 33 percent.

"A Short History of Bull Markets,"
Forbes Magazine (6/19/95)

So what does constitute a bull market? My review of the stock
market in the twentieth century shows many fluctuations of 10 or
15 percent that didn't develop into anything beyond that. When
stocks as measured by the Dow Jones Industrial Average *and* the
Standard & Poor's (S&P) 500 Stock Price Index rise to **+19 percent,** that is the threshold from which advances have then risen 96
percent of the time to over +29 percent. The "mini"-bull markets
lasting an average of 3.2 months and rising less than 40 points on
average are excluded from this tabulation, which eliminates the
10 aberrations of the 1930s. (Details can be found in Chapter 7.)

Half of the "official" bull markets have risen over 80 percent
with the average gain of bull markets being +115 percent and
lasting 34 months based on the record with the aberrations of the
1930s removed. In the twentieth century, 100 percent of those bull
markets were accompanied by or followed shortly after their start
by economic expansions, as shown in Table 3.5.

Charles Dow originally developed his "average" not only as a
measure of the stock market's daily fluctuations but as a guide to
future economic activity. Indeed, today the Conference Board
uses the S&P 500 as one of its components in its Index of Leading
Economic Indicators.

Figure 5.1 shows the 25 bull markets of the twentieth and twenty-
first centuries; Table 5.1 lists the data used to compile Figure 5.1.
It is important to identify bull markets as soon as possible because
the first year is usually the strongest with the best chance of profitable investment results: an average +45.7 percent gain, and 84 percent of bull markets complete that first year. Then the gains, while
still positive, do drop off as a percentage in the next two years. Only
36 percent of bull markets complete the third year. But curiously,
of the nine that did complete their third year, eight (89 percent)
went on to complete their fourth year! Perhaps this percentage and
the +19.5 percent average advance are a reflection of being the
last leg in the bull market and/or a reaction to no recession having

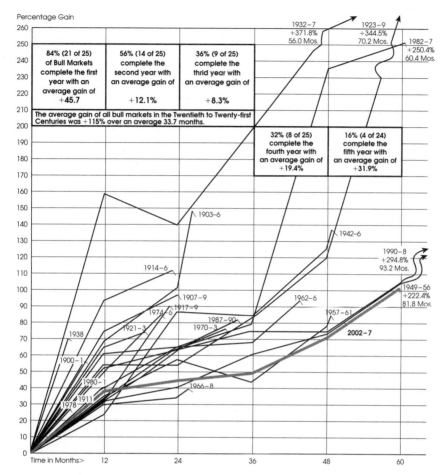

Percentage Gain

| 84% (21 of 25) of Bull Markets complete the first year with an average gain of +45.7 | 56% (14 of 25) complete the second year with an average gain of +12.1% | 36% (9 of 25) complete the thrid year with an average gain of +8.3% |

The average gain of all bull markets in the Twentieth to Twenty-first Centuries was +115% over an average 33.7 months.

32% (8 of 25) complete the fourth year with an average gain of +19.4%

16% (4 of 24) complete the fifth year with an average gain of +31.9%

1932–7 +371.8% 56.0 Mos.

1923–9 +344.5% 70.2 Mos.

1982–7 +250.4% 60.4 Mos.

1903–6

1914–6

1938

1907–9

1917–9

1974–6

1921–3

1987–90

1970–3

1900–1

1980–1

1911

1978

1966–8

1942–6

1962–6

1957–61

2002–7

1990–8 +294.8% 93.2 Mos.

1949–56 +222.4% 81.8 Mos.

Time in Months>   12   24   36   48   60

Figure 5.1   Bull Markets of the Twentieth and Twenty-First Centuries

appeared to that point, as might have been expected. Some things in the stock market happen without explanation, and this may be one of them.

Even *after* the time bull markets become "official," significant further gains occur on average, as shown in Table 5.2.

Other interesting statistics can be gleaned from the bell curve of bull markets shown in Figure 5.2.

As you can see from the figures and tables, the shortest and longest bull markets were 5.9 months (in 2001–2) and 93.2 months

Table 5.1 Bull Market Gains, 1900 to 2007, Excluding Dividends

Bear Low	Level	1 Year Later	% Gain	2 Years Later	% Gain	3 Years Later	% Gain	4 Years Later	% Gain	5 Years Later	% Gain
9/24/1900	52.96	n/a									
11/9/1903	42.15	67.07	59.1	81.56	21.6	n/a					
11/15/1907	53.00	88.09	66.2	99.31	12.7	n/a					
9/25/1911	72.94	93.38	28.0	n/a							
12/24/1914	53.17	98.36	85.0	n/a							
12/19/1917	65.95	82.40	24.9	n/a							
8/24/1921	63.90	99.71	56.0	n/a							
10/27/1923	85.76	101.73	18.6	152.92	50.3	151.87	-0.7	183.96	21.1	255.51	+38.9
7/8/1932	41.22	105.15	155.1	97.15	-7.6	122.55	26.1	156.1	27.4	n/a	
3/31/1938	98.95	n/a									
4/28/1942	92.92	134.14	44.4	136.21	1.5	164.71	20.9	206.13	25.1	n/a	
6/13/1949	161.60	226.44	40.1	250.03	10.4	268.56	7.4	265.78	-1.0	322.09	+21.2
10/22/1957	419.79	542.31	29.2	625.59	15.4	582.69	-6.9	705.62	21.1	n/a	
6/26/1962	535.76	709.00	32.3	830.99	17.2	854.36	2.8	n/a			
10/7/1966	744.32	928.74	24.8	956.68	3.0	n/a					
5/26/1970	631.16	906.41	43.6	971.25	7.2	n/a					
12/6/1974	577.60	818.80	41.8	n/a							
2/28/1978	742.12	n/a									
4/21/1980	759.13	1005.94	32.5	n/a							
8/12/1982	776.92	1182.83	52.2	1218.09	3.0	1314.29	7.9	1835.49	39.7	2669.32	+45.4
10/19/1987	1738.74	2137.27	22.9	2683.2	25.5	n/a					
10/11/1990	2365.10	2983.68	26.2	3136.58	5.1	3593.41	14.6	3876.83	7.9	4735.20	+22.1
8/31/1998	7539.07	10829.28	43.6	n/a							
9/21/2001	8235.81	n/a									
10/9/2002	7286.27	9680.01	32.9	10055.20	3.9	10292.31	2.4	11857.81	15.2	14164.53	19.5
		21 of 25 (84%) complete 1st year	Average gain: +45.7	14 of 25 (56%) complete 2nd year	Average gain: +12.1	9 of 25 (36%) complete 3rd year	Average gain: +8.3	8 of 25 (32%) complete 4th year	Average gain: +19.5	5 of 25 (20%) complete 5th year	Average gain +29.4

Table 5.2 "Official" Bull Markets (+19%) and the S&P 500 Gain (data since January 1, 1949)

"Official" Bull Markets (+19%) and the S&P 500 Gain Thereafter:

Date	Level	3 Months Level	Gain	6 Months Level	Gain	9 Months Level	Gain	1 year Level	Gain	To "official" Bear Market (−16%) Date	Level	Gain
11/2/1949	16.33	17.23	5.5%	18.11	10.9%	17.95	9.9%	19.73	20.8%	10/17/1957	40.65	148.9%
7/25/1958	46.97	50.81	8.2%	56.00	19.2%	57.96	23.4%	59.65	27.0%	5/25/1962	59.47	26.6%
11/29/1962	62.41	64.29	3.0%	70.01	12.2%	72.04	15.4%	73.23	17.3%	8/22/1966	78.24	25.4%
4/24/1967	92.62	93.73	1.2%	94.42	1.9%	93.17	0.6%	96.62	4.3%	7/28/1969	90.21	−2.6%
9/4/1970	82.83	89.46	8.0%	97.92	18.2%	101.30	22.3%	100.69	21.6%	8/21/1973	100.89	21.8%
2/3/1975	77.82	89.22	14.6%	87.99	13.1%	89.04	14.4%	100.87	29.6%	1/10/1978	90.17	15.9%
8/3/1978	103.51	96.18	−7.1%	99.50	−3.9%	101.81	−1.6%	104.04	0.5%	3/26/1980	98.68	−4.7%
7/14/1980	120.01	132.02	10.0%	133.47	11.2%	132.68	10.6%	129.65	8.0%	9/23/1981	115.65	−3.6%
9/3/1982	122.68	138.69	13.1%	153.48	25.1%	164.42	34.0%	165.00	34.5%	10/16/1987	282.70	133.3%
2/29/1988	267.82	253.42	−5.4%	262.33	−2.0%	270.91	1.2%	288.86	7.9%	8/23/1990	307.06	14.7%
2/6/1991	358.07	380.08	6.1%	390.62	9.1%	389.97	8.9%	408.79	14.2%	8/31/1998	957.28	167.3%
11/6/1998	1141.01	1239.40	8.6%	1332.05	16.7%	1300.29	14.0%	1370.23	20.1%	3/16/2001	1150.53	0.8%
11/19/2001	1151.06	1083.3	−5.9%	1106.59	−3.9%	920.47*	−20.0%			7/10/2002	920.47	−20.0%
11/21/2002	933.76	848.17	−9.2%	923.42	−1.1%	1003.27	7.4%	1035.28	10.9%	3/7/2008	1293.37	38.5%
Ave:			3.6%		9.1%		10.0%		16.7%			

Average Annual Gain Buy to Sell: 12.8% including dividends

*This bull market became an "official" bear market on 7/10/02 at 920.47.

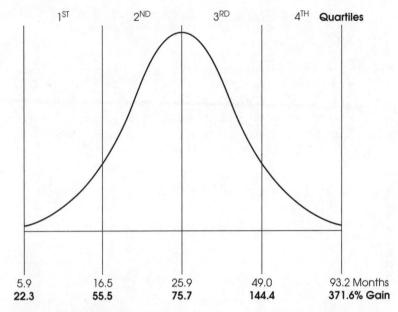

1ST	2ND	3RD	4TH	**Quartiles**

5.9	16.5	25.9	49.0	93.2 Months
22.3	55.5	75.7	144.4	371.6% Gain

Figure 5.2   Bell Curve of the Length and Gain of Previous Bull Markets (25 Bull Markets)

(from 1990 to 1998) respectively. The least gain was 22.3 percent and the most gain was 371.6 percent. The median of all 24 complete bull markets was a 75.7 percent gain, and it lasted 25.9 months. This statistical information provides you with a historic perspective of where any particular bull market stands in relation to others and the status of a current bull market. Bull (or bear) markets can end at any point, but the quartiles show the odds of when they might end.

Economic Predictor of Business Activity

The Dow Jones Industrial Average developed by Charles H. Dow in 1895 and the Railroad (now Transportation) Average added in 1897 *were originally intended to be indicators of business activity.* It is said that the market is always looking ahead, and when it (the combined "vision" of all investors) sees good business ahead, it will go up. By adding the "official" bull definition, you can see that the market has been an excellent predictor of the economy in the twentieth and twenty-first centuries, as shown in Table 5.3.

One hundred percent of bull markets in the twentieth and twenty-first centuries have been accompanied, or followed shortly thereafter (4.3 months on average), by economic expansions. So events over the years since the introduction of his theory have pretty well proven Charles Dow's expectation that the stock market does "predict" future business activity.

Table 5.3   Stock Market as a Business Cycle Predictor: Bull Markets and Expansions

Bull Market Dates (mo/yr)	Business Expansions	Expansion in Years	Lead Time of Bull Market Start to Expansion
9/1900–6/01	12/00–9/02	1.8	3 months
11/03–1/06	8/04–5/07	2.8	9
11/07–11/09	6/08–1/10	1.4	7
9/11–9/12	1/12–1/13	1.0	4
7/14–11/16	12/14–8/18	3.7	5
12/17–11/19	3/19–1/20	.8	15
8/21–3/23	7/21–5/23	1.8	−1
10/23–9/29	7/24–10/26	2.3	9
	(11/27–8/29)	1.8	n/a
7/32–3/37	3/33–5/37	4.2	8
3/38–11/38	6/38–2/45	6.7	3
4/42–5/46	See above		n/a
	(10/45–11/48)	3.1	n/a
6/49–4/56	10/49–7/53	3.75	4
	(5/54–8/57)	3.25	n/a
10/57–12/61	4/58–4/60	2.0	6
6/62–2/66	2/61–12/66*	5.8	−16
10/66–12/68	6/67*–12/69	2.5	8
5/70–1/73	11/70–11/73	3.0	6
12/74–9/76	3/75–1/80	4.8	3
2/78–9/78	See above		n/a
4/80–4/81	7/80–7/81	1.0	3
8/82–8/87	11/82–7/90	7.7	3
10/87–7/90	See above		n/a
10/90–7/98	3/91–3/01	10.0	5
8/98–1/2000	See above		n/a
9/01–3/02	11/01–12/07?	6.1 to date	2
10/02–10/07	See above		n/a
Average: Expansion is 3.4 years and lead time is 4.3 Months			

*According to *Forbes* magazine (January 23, 1989), the economic expansion was interrupted by a "growth recession" when industrial production fell from the first quarter to the third quarter of 1967.

CHAPTER 6

Bear Markets

Bull markets are always followed by bear markets. They say "no tree grows to the sky," and that's just a way of saying that bull markets do not continue indefinitely. Nothing lasts forever. Just as the other side of a coin from heads is tails, so too do we have bear markets. At any given time, most investors have some money invested in the stock market, and hope for higher prices is the prevailing attitude. That is one reason it is so hard to accept the arrival, never mind predict the arrival, of bear markets. However, they are a normal part of the stock market's cycles. In this chapter, we identify them and discuss their consequences for the economy and their impact on investor's fortunes.

Bear Markets in the Twentieth and Twenty-First Centuries

Just like bull markets, bear markets also tend to have various definitions. Bear markets have been defined as:

A **9 percent** drop (if followed by a recession)	*Money Magazine* (October 1998)
A **13 percent** drop (after 155 days)	Ned Davis Research in the *Wall Street Journal* (3/20/95)
A **15 percent** drop	David L. Babson & Co. in the *White Mountain Independent* (9/4/98), *Wall Street Journal* (1/27/95), and *Forbes* (6/12/00) on the S&P

	Schannep Timing Indicator and
A 16 percent drop on both the Dow Jones and the S&P 500 over any time frame	**TheDowTheory.com Newsletter (1995)**
An **18 percent** drop on the S&P 500	Standard & Poor's (3/25/01)
A **20 percent** drop on the Dow Jones	Dow Jones & Co: *Wall Street Journal* (10/12/90), the day of the Desert Storm bear market low
A **20 percent** drop (over at least three months)	*Wall Street Journal* (11/28/94) after Desert Storm
A **20 to 25 percent** drop	Morgan Stanley Dean Witter (8/13/98)
A **22 to 23 percent** drop	State Street Research in the *Wall Street Journal* (9/11/98)
A **30 percent** drop (after 50 days)	Ned Davis Research in the *Wall Street Journal* (3/20/95)
"'A lot' of stocks going down 'a lot' over a long period of time"	Morgan Stanley Dean Witter (12/3/98)
"A long downward movement interrupted by important rallies"	Robert Rhea, *The Dow Theory* (1932)

No wonder there is confusion about bear markets. Some definitions require that you wait for several months, or for however long it takes to see if there is going to be a recession. Usually—over 70 percent of the time in the case of my definition—bear markets "forecast" recessions. Since bear markets and recessions usually go hand in hand with bear markets leading the way, let's make sure we have a firm understanding of what recessions are. Most people think a recession is when there are two successive quarters of negative Gross National Product. Actually, the National Bureau of Economic Research (NBER), the official arbiter for determining when recessions start and end, has a different view, as you can see at their website www.nber.org. They define a recession as a "significant decline in economic activity spread across the economy, lasting more than a few months, normally visible in real GDP, real income, employment, industrial production, and wholesale-retail sales." Further they state that "a recession—the way we use the word—is a period of *diminishing* activity, rather than *diminished* activity."

Waiting for the "traditional" 20 percent definition of a bear market to be met has resulted in several bear markets *and* recessions being missed. The 1923 bear market (−18.6 percent) and its *following recession*, the 1956–57 bear market (−19.4 percent) and its *following recession*, and the 1978 to 1980 bear market (−16.4 percent) and its *following recession were all missed*. Even the *Wall Street Journal*

(10/21/29) referred to 1923's –18.6 percent drop as "a genuine major Bear market." Since 1946, the *Wall Street Journal*'s definition of –20 percent for the Dow has identified only *11* of the last 14 bear markets that preceded six recessions. Standard & Poor's definition of –18 percent for the S&P identified *12* of the last 14 that preceded seven recessions. My definition of –16 percent on both the Dow Jones and S&P 500 identified *all 14* that preceded eight recessions.

The *Journal* has further stated that "there is no formal way to define bull and bear markets" (12/15/98). I disagree.

The stock market has had declines of *10 percent* some 50 to 100 times in the twentieth century, yet not all resulted in bear markets. In addition to being an excellent forecasting tool for predicting recessions when using my definition of bear markets, the threshold of –16 percent has resulted nearly 80 percent of the time in *declines of at least –24 percent.* The "mini"–bull markets lasting an average of 3.2 months and rising less than 40 points on average are excluded from this tabulation, which eliminates the 10 aberrations of the 1930s. *The average loss for bear markets has been –34* percent *over a year and a half* average time frame. Over the last 100 years, 71 percent of the time, the –16 percent definition has been followed by a recession. It happens that –16 percent is the reciprocal of a 19 percent advance (and vice versa), which is my definition of a bull market. It takes a 19 percent gain to make up for a –16 percent loss. Figure 6.1 shows the 24 previous bear markets of the twentieth and twenty–first centuries.

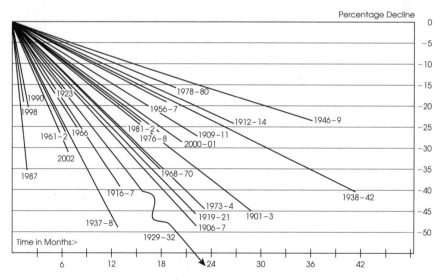

Figure 6.1   Bear Markets in the Twentieth and Twenty-First Centuries

Figure 6.1 shows the percentage loss (extent) and time in months (duration) of the bear markets over the last 100 years. The data for each will be shown in the next chapter. This graphic presentation shows a straight line to the ending point, but don't get the idea that that was the actual pattern of those individual bear markets. As Charles Dow's successor, William Peter Hamilton, once commented, "On Dow's old theory . . . the secondary rallies in a bear market are *sudden and rapid.* . . . " No bear market goes down without a fight.

Table 6.1 shows what happens after a bear market becomes "official." As you can see, by the time bear markets become "official," the majority of the decline has happened, although, on average, another 12 percent drop occurs over the following four to six months. Eight of the last 10 recessions were signaled by bear markets, while two were not. Eight of the last 14 bear markets signaled recessions, but six did not.

Table 6.1   Official Bear Markets (−16% on Both the DJIA & S&P 500) and the Further S&P 500 Loss to the Final Lows (Data since January 1, 1946)

Date of −16%	Level	Further loss	Months	Date	Level	Recession?
			Final Bear Market Lows			
9/4/1946	15.46	12.4%	33.3	6/13/1949	13.55	**YES**
10/17/1957	40.65	4.1%	0.6	10/22/1957	38.98	**YES**
5/25/1962	59.47	12.0%	1.0	6/26/1962	52.32	NO
8/22/1966	78.24	6.4%	1.5	10/7/1966	73.20	NO
7/28/1969	90.21	23.2%	10.0	5/26/1970	69.29	**YES**
8/21/1973	100.89	38.3%	14.5	10/3/1974	62.28	**YES**
1/10/1978	90.17	3.6%	1.9	3/6/1978	86.90	NO
3/26/1980	98.68	0.5%	0.0	3/27/1980	98.22	**YES**
9/23/1981	115.65	11.4%	10.7	8/12/1982	102.42	**YES**
10/16/1987	282.70	20.8%	1.6	12/4/1987	223.92	NO
8/23/1990	307.06	3.8%	1.6	10/11/1990	295.46	**YES**
8/31/1998	957.28	0.0%	0.0	8/31/1998	957.28	NO
3/16/2001	1150.53	16.1%	6.2	9/21/2001	965.80	**YES**
7/10/2002	920.47	15.6%	2.0	10/9/2002	776.76	NO
3/7/2008						
	Average:	12%	6.1			

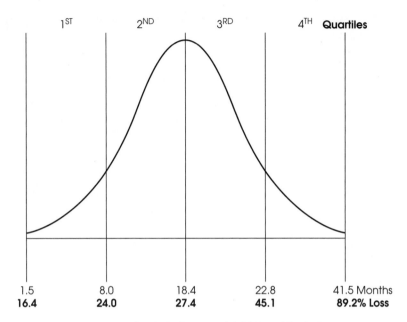

Figure 6.2   Bell Curve of 24 Bear Markets

Other interesting statistics can be gleaned from the bell curve of bear markets shown in Figure 6.2.

As you can see from the figures and tables, the shortest bear market lasted only 1.5 months and the longest lasted 41.5 months. The smallest decline was 16.4 percent, the largest decline was 89.2 percent. The median of all 23 complete bear markets was a 27.4 percent decline and lasted 18.4 months. Current markets can be plotted on these bell curves to get an idea of where they may be in their life cycle and the odds of continuance.

Stock Market as a Business Cycle Predictor

Table 6.2 shows that the last 24 bear markets have been followed by 17 recessions (71 percent of the time), 9.6 months on average after a bear market started. The stock market's movements are, of course, dictated by the resultant buying and selling of its participants and this table seems to confirm that they know what they are doing. By adding the "official" bear definition, you can see that "the market" has been an excellent predictor of the stock market and recessions in the twentieth and twenty–first centuries.

Table 6.2   Stock Market as a Business Cycle Predictor: Bear Markets and Recessions

Bear Market Dates	Recessions	Recession in Months	Bear Market Start to Recession Start: Lead Time in Months	% Drop before Recession	Total Bear Market Drop
6/1901–11/03	9/02–8/04	23	15	–15%	46.1%
1/06–11/07	5/07–6/08	13	16	–21	48.5
11/09–9/11	1/10–1/12	24	2	–6	27.4
9/12–7/14	1/13–12/14	23	4	–10	24.6
11/16–12/17	8/18– 3/19	7	21	–25	40.1
11/19–8/21	1/20–7/21	18	2	–13	46.6
3/23–10/23	5/23–7/24	14	2	–8	18.6
	(10/26–11/27)	13	n/a	n/a	n/a
9/29–7/32	8/29–3/33*	43	–1	0	89.2
3/37–3/38	5/37–6/38	13	2	–11	49.1
11/38–4/42	None		n/a	n/a	41.3
	(2/45–10/45)	8	n/a	n/a	n/a
5/46–6/49	11/48–10/49	11	30	–17	24.0
	(7/53–5/54)	10	n/a	n/a	n/a
4/56–10/57	8/57–4/58	8	16	–7	19.4
	(4/60–2/61)	10	n/a	n/a	n/a
12/61–6/62	None/"mild"		n/a	n/a	27.1
2/66–10/66	None/but…†		n/a	n/a	25.2
12/68–5/70	12/69–11/70	11	12	–19	35.9
1/73–12/74	11/73– 3/75	16	10	–15	45.1
9/76– 2/78	None		n/a	n/a	26.9
9/78– 4/80	1/80–7/80	6	16	–3	16.4
4/81– 8/82	7/81–11/82	16	3	–6	24.1
8/87–10/87	None		n/a	n/a	36.1
7/90–10/90	7/90–3/91	8	0	0	21.2
7/98–8/98	None		n/a	n/a	19.3
1/2000–3/01	3/01–11/01	8	14	–7	29.7
3/02–10/02	None		n/a	n/a	31.5
10/07					
	Average	**14.4 mos.**	**9.6 mos.**	**–10.8%**	**33.9%**

*Depression.
†Growth recession per *Forbes* magazine (1/23/89): Industrial production fell from first-quarter 1967 to third-quarter 1967.

Table 6.3   Frequency of Bear Markets and Recessions

35-Year Time Frame	Number of Bear Markets	Number of Recessions
1901–1935	8	9
1936–1970	7	7
1971–2006	9	5

The bottom line is that 71 percent of bear markets since 1900 have been followed by recessions. But this is a case of the "average" occurrence concealing what is actually happening. As shown in Table 6.3, if you divide the last 105 years into three 35-year periods, you'll see a different picture emerging.

As you can see, the number of bear markets per period is quite constant; however, the number of recessions has diminished considerably. For instance, eight bear markets and nine recessions started in the first period from 1901 to 1935. In the 1936 to 1970 period, seven bear markets and seven recessions began. In the most recent period from 1971 to 2006, there were nine bear markets but only five recessions started. In other words, the frequency of bear markets stayed rather steady at about one every 4.33 years, but the occurrence of recessions went from one every four years to only one every seven years in the recent period. And bear markets became less predictive of recession: from 11 of the first 12 (92 percent) bear markets being followed by recession to only 6 of the most recent 12 (50 percent) bear markets being followed by recession. Therefore, recessions are not such a frequent threat to the economy, but bear markets continue to haunt investors from time to time, just as they always have. Of the 21 total recessions, only the four recessions shown in parentheses in Table 6.2 were not tied to bear markets in any way.

Now that we have completed our review of both bull and bear markets, the next chapter puts them together into a combined record.

Bull and Bear Markets of the Twentieth and Twenty-First Centuries

In his short life, Charles Dow developed an understanding that went beyond just the Dow Jones Industrial Average and the Dow Jones Transportation Average. He had an understanding of human nature. A quote from Charles Dow (June 8, 1901) that captures an attitude that many people unfortunately harbor follows:

> There is always a disposition in people's minds to think that existing conditions will be permanent. When the market is down and dull, it's hard to make people believe that this is the prelude to a period of activity and advance. When prices are up and the country is prosperous, it is always said that while preceding booms have not lasted, there are circumstances connected with this one which make it unlike its predecessors and give assurance of permanency. The one fact pertaining to all conditions is that they will change.

In this chapter, you will see how change is manifested the stock market.

A History of Bull and Bear Markets

In the stock market, there is no greater change than from a bull market to a bear market and then the reverse, the change from bear to bull. Using the definitions for bull and bear markets that I introduced in Chapters 5 and 6, we can now put them together into an "official" record. Bull markets must rise at least +19 percent on both the Dow Jones Industrials and the Standard & Poor's (S&P) 500 Index to qualify. Bear markets must lose at least –16 percent on both averages. The phrase "stocks tend to fluctuate" was attributed to J. P. Morgan in one of history's great understatements. One look at the history of the stock market in the twentieth and twenty-first centuries confirms this. The stock market has bull and bear cycles that offer opportunities for profit if you recognize them and are on the right side of them. The history that follows shows the duration and magnitude of gain in the case of bull markets and loss in the case of bear markets. While no two markets are ever the same, history can be a guide to what to expect.

Table 7.1 shows the high and low dates, the Dow Jones Industrial Average (DJIA) levels, gain or loss percentage, and the number of months involved for each of the 25 bull markets and 24 bear markets of this and the last century.

As shown in Table 7.1, bull markets more than doubled on average in just under three years. Bear markets dropped one-third on average in a year and a half. Historically the stock market has been in a bull market 67 percent of the time and in bear markets 33 percent of the time. For the last 17 years of the twentieth century, the percentages were 97 and 3 percent, but that was unique and you should not have expected that to continue. The prior 16 years were split almost exactly 50–50. Since the start of the twenty-first century, the markets have returned to the more normal 67 percent of the time in bull markets and 33 percent in bear markets.

Charles Dow had thought that a complete cycle of bull and bear would last 10 years, 5 years as a bull and 5 years as a bear. With the passing of time and with more market history to rely on, it is obvious that his assumption was incorrect. Anyone who has read *Future Shock* knows that things happen faster now

Table 7.1   Bull and Bear Markets of the Twentieth and Twenty-First Centuries

| Low Date | High Date | DJIA | 25 Bull Markets (+19%)* | | 24 Bear Markets (−16%)* | |
			% Gain*	No. of Months	% Loss*	No. of Months
9/24/1900		52.96				
	6/17/01	78.26	47.8	8.7		
11/9/03		42.15			46.1	28.7
	1/19/06	103.00	144.4	26.3		
11/15/07		53.00			48.5	21.9
	11/19/09	100.53	89.7	24.1		
9/25/11		72.94			27.4	22.2
	9/30/12	94.15	29.1	12.2		
12/24/14	(was 73.48)	53.17	< (basis changed)		24.6	26.8
	11/21/16	110.15	107.2	22.9		
12/19/17		65.95			40.1	13.0
	11/3/19	119.62	81.4	22.5		
8/24/21		63.90			46.6	21.7
	3/20/23	105.38	64.9	18.9		
10/27/23		85.76			18.6	7.2
	9/3/29	381.17	344.5	70.2		
7/8/32		41.22			89.2	34.2
	3/10/37	194.40	371.6	56.0		
3/31/38		98.95			49.1	12.7
	11/12/38	158.41	60.1	7.4		
4/28/42		92.92			41.3	41.5
	5/29/46	212.50	128.7	49.0		
6/13/49		161.60			24.0	36.5
	4/6/56	521.05	222.4	81.8		
10/22/57		419.79			19.4	18.5
	12/13/61	734.91	75.1	49.7		
6/26/62		535.76			27.1	6.4
	2/9/66	995.15	85.7	43.4		
10/7/66		744.32			25.2	8.0
	12/3/68	985.21	32.4	25.9		
5/26/70		631.16			35.9	17.8
	1/11/73	1051.70	66.6	31.5		
12/6/74		577.60			45.1	22.8
	9/21/76	1014.79	75.7	21.5		

(continued)

Table 7.1 *(continued)*

Low Date	High Date	DJIA	25 Bull Markets (+19%)*		24 Bear Markets (−16%)*	
			% Gain*	No. of Months	% Loss*	No. of Months
2/28/78		742.12			26.9	17.2
	9/11/78	907.74	22.3	6.4		
4/21/80		759.13			16.4	19.3
	4/27/81	1024.05	34.9	13.2		
8/12/82		776.92			24.1	15.5
	8/25/87	2722.42	250.4	60.4		
10/19/87		1738.74			36.1	1.8
	7/16/90	2999.75	72.5	32.9		
10/11/90		2365.10			21.2	2.8
	7/17/98	9337.97	294.8	93.2		
8/31/98		7539.07			19.3	1.5
	1/14/00	11722.98	55.5	16.5		
9/21/01		8235.81			29.7	20.2
	3/19/02	10635.25	29.1	5.9		
10/9/02		7286.27			31.5	6.7
	10/9/07	14164.53	94.5	60.0		
Average:			**+115.4%**	**34.3 months**	**−33.7%**	**17.6 months**

0–9% = Fluctuation	−9 to −16% = Correction*	−16% = Bear market
	+9 to +19% = Rally*	+19% = Bull market

*Percentages must be attained on *both* the DJIA and the S&P 500.

than 100 years ago. For instance, in a little over one year, from September 2001 to October 2002, there was a complete bull/bear cycle. When the bear market ended in capitulation just 10 days after the 9/11 tragedy there was a brief but real bull market lasting just short of six months, rising 2400 Dow points, +29.1 percent on the Dow Jones. And then a seven-month bear market lost −31.5 percent and also ended in capitulation in October 2002, after which another bull market began. That bull market lasted a full five years, so if a following bear market also lasts five years, then it may yet prove Charles Dow's original idea correct. But more likely it will be a normal bear market lasting from one to two years.

The Aberrations

The 10 "mini"–bull markets shown in Table 7.2 were aberrations in the 1930s, lasting an average of three months and 40 points. They are excluded for the purpose of definitions and the record but shown here to complete the unabridged record.

Figure 7.1 shows bull markets in white, bear markets in black, and recessions in gray. The best possible investment results would be obtained from being on-board during all the white periods and out of the market during all the black times. We all know that is not attainable, but that does not stop us from trying. What is also evident is that the long-standing correlation of the stock market typically "predicting" economic recessions is valid and will, no doubt, continue in the twenty-first century.

Table 7.2   10 "Mini"–Bull Markets

Lows	Highs	DJIA	% Gain	No. of Months	% Loss	No. of Months
11/13/1929		198.69			47.9	2.3
	4/17/30	294.07	48.0	5.1		
12/16/30		157.51			46.4	8.0
	2/24/31	194.36	23.4	2.3		
6/2/31		121.70			37.4	3.2
	6/27/31	156.93	28.9	.8		
10/5/31		86.48			44.3	3.1
	11/9/31	116.79	35.0	1.1		
1/5/32		71.24			39.0	1.8
	3/8/32	88.78	24.6	2.1		
7/18/32		41.22			53.6	4.0
	9/7/32	79.93	93.9	2.0		
2/27/33		50.16			37.2	5.7
	7/18/33	108.67	116.6	4.6		
10/21/33		83.64			23.0	3.1
	2/5/34	110.74	32.4	3.5		
7/26/34		85.51			22.8	5.6
4/8/39		121.44			23.3	4.9
	9/12/39	155.92	28.4	5.1		
6/10/40		111.84			28.3	8.9
	11/9/40	138.12	23.5	5.0		
4/28/42		92.92			32.7	17.7

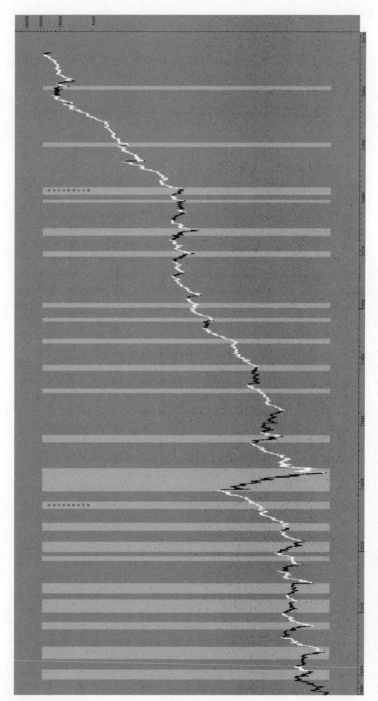

Figure 7.1   Bull and Bear Markets and Recessions From 1897-2008

This chapter serves as a reference point for bull and bear markets in the future. We cannot predict their duration and magnitude, but we can count on their recurrence! Realizing that bull and bear markets are repeated over time and that participating in bull markets and avoiding bear markets is the ultimate goal of successful investing, we'll proceed in the next several chapters to focus on improved ways of predicting both bull and bear markets.

THE DOW THEORY FOR THE TWENTY-FIRST CENTURY

Capitulation: The Selling Climax

In this chapter, we look at one of the most frightening times in the stocks market's cycle and at the same time one of the most profitable times to get back into the market. Initially I show you what capitulation is and the specific dates that I have been able to identify it. The first, in 1962, was found through backtesting, but those since then were shown in real time. After this introduction to capitulation, I present a formal paper outlining the eight best indicators and their record in identifying capitulation.

Capitulation: The Time to Buy

Capitulation as it relates to the stock market is when investors and speculators throw in the towel because they are so disheartened, fearful, need to meet margin calls, or whatever. It is often called a "selling climax" as stocks cascade down into a cataclysmic sell-off.

When Dow, Hamilton, and Rhea wrote about the market and the Dow Theory in particular, they never mentioned the word "capitulation," but it was clearly alluded to when Robert Rhea wrote "the third [phase of a bear market] is caused by distress selling of sound securities, regardless of their value, by those who must find a cash market for at least a portion of their assets." He went on to say, "After a market has drastically declined . . . and then goes into a semi-panic collapse it is wise to cover short positions and even perhaps make commitments for long accounts."

Many market observers identify capitulation only after it has happened, but that need not be the case. A *definite and measurable level of capitulation* often occurs at or near market lows. Of the *11* times that capitulation has met the defined levels in my database, *3* have been on the day of the Bear market low; *5* others have been *within one to three days* of lows and within 2 percent of the lows. *Two* preceded the first lows of double bottoms and were followed by second capitulations, which marked the final lows, and *1* was 35 days early and 5 percent above the ultimate low. The average of the 11 was within 3.2 percent of the low close on the Dow Jones Industrial Average and/or the Standard & Poor's 500 Index. Such capitulation can be used to "make commitments for long account" with an initial purchase prior to the traditional Dow Theory buy signal. I have no doubt that Charles Dow would have welcomed the discovery of such a way to clearly identify the "semi-panic collapse" he observed.

Since a traditional Dow Theory buy signal has *always* followed capitulation, the parameters of the Dow Theory can be interpreted in shorter time frames, resulting in a buy signal average entry level that is closer to the lows than more stringent interpretation would otherwise allow. Examples of bear markets ending in capitulation can be found in June 1962, May 1970, August and September 1974, October and December 1987, August 1990, August 1998, September 2001, and July and October 2002. No doubt other capitulations occurred before 1954, but that is the earliest year that my personal database covers with the necessary calculations. The next section gives the specifics of the 11 signals.

About Capitulation

A number of systems have tried to turn the generality of capitulation into a specific identification, as you will see in the formal paper on capitulation presented in the next section. The fact is, capitulation can be measured and identified quite specifically. I show that *partial* capitulation occurred 14 times since my database began in 1953, with 11 going on to *total* capitulation within days. The three that failed to *completely* capitulate were on 12/5/73, 3/27/80, and 3/21/01, and the aftermath of those were quite good. But *total* capitulation was reached only 11 times, as shown in Table 8.1, and

Table 8.1   Capitulations and Their Aftermaths

Date	Trading Days before the Bear Market Lows (DJIA)	Percent above Lows	Next Bull Market Advance	Length of Bull Market
6/22/62	2	0.5%	+85.7%	43.4 months
5/25/70	1	1.6	+66.6	31.5
8/23/74	74 (27 days before the S&P500 low)	18.9 (14.9 above S&P low)	+75.7	21.5
also 9/30/74	50 (3 days before the S&P500 low)	5.2 (2.0 above S&P low)	+75.7	21.5
10/19/87	0 (*the* low)	0.0	+72.5	32.9
also 12/3/87	34 *after* (1 day before S&P low)	2.2 (0.6 above S&P low)	+72.5	32.9
8/23/90	35	5.0	+294.8	93.3
8/31/98	0 (*the* low)	0.0	+55.5	16.5
9/20/01	1	1.7	+29.1	5.9
7/19/02	57 (2 before 1st low)	9.1 to final bottom	+94.5	60.0
also 10/9/02	0 (*the* low)	0.0	+94.5	60.0
Average:	11.5 days (Dow and/or S&P low)	3.2 % (Dow Jones and/or S&P low)	+92.5%	38.1 months
Median:	1–2 days	1.6%	+75.5%	32.2 months

those times averaged within 3.2 percent of the lows and 12 days ahead of the bear market lows.

Every bear market ends differently. Some end with a whimper, but even those that terminate in a capitulation do so in varying patterns. Figures 8.1 to 8.8 show those bottoms that were accompanied by capitulation, including the three that had double capitulations. Some are actually at the low point, and all are at least near the low point. Obviously, these are the times when you would want to have the courage, means, and indications for when to invest in the stock market. (I am profoundly thankful to Jonathan Stein for producing these and other charts used in the text.)

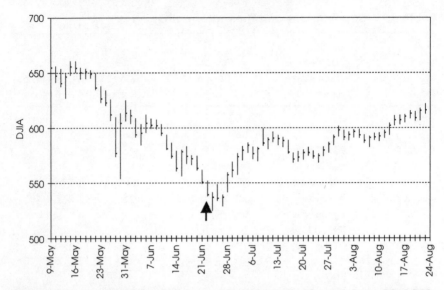

Figure 8.1 Capitulation Points and the Market's Moves: June 22, 1962

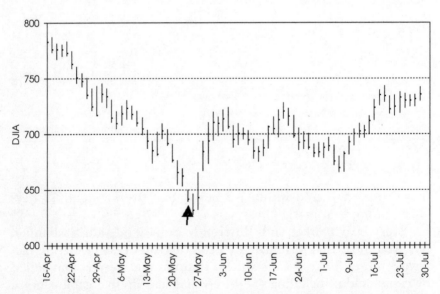

Figure 8.2 Capitulation Points and the Market's Moves: May 25, 1970

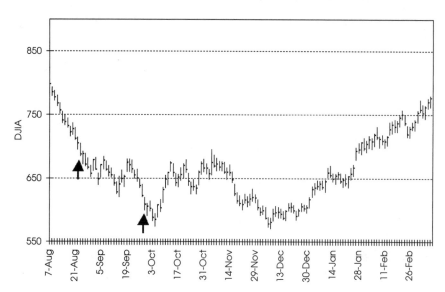

**Figure 8.3   Double Capitulation Points and the Market's Moves:
August 2 and September 30, 1974**

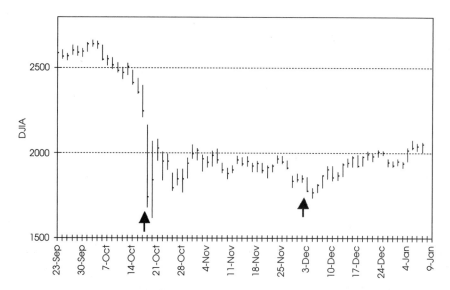

**Figure 8.4   Double Capitulation Points and the Market's Moves:
October 19 and December 3, 1987**

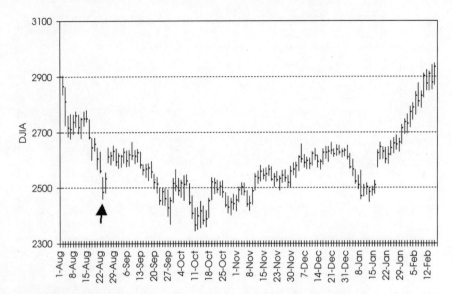

**Figure 8.5   Capitulation Points and the Market's Moves:
August 23, 1990**

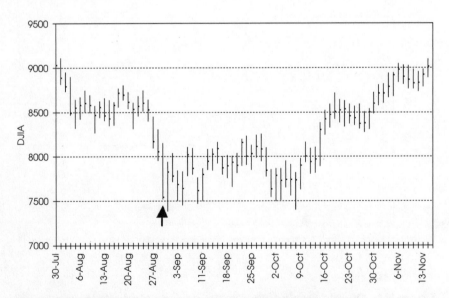

**Figure 8.6   Capitulation Points and the Market's Moves:
August 31, 1998**

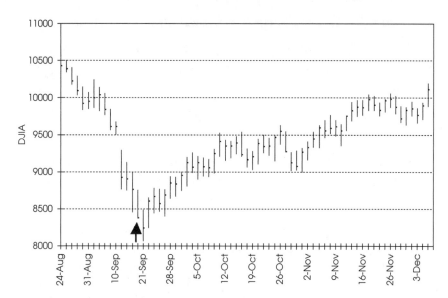

**Figure 8.7   Capitulation Points and the Market's Moves:
September 20, 2001**

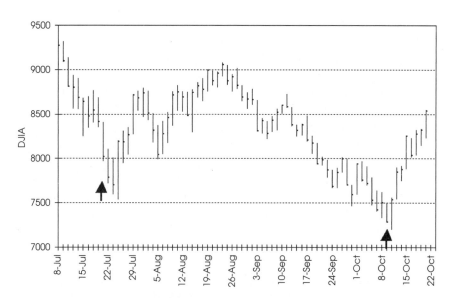

**Figure 8.8   Double Capitulation Points and the Market's Moves:
July 19 and October 9, 2002**

Formal Paper Submitted Concerning Capitulation

A reprint of a paper that I submitted to the Market Technicians Association in the Charles H. Dow Award competition in 2005 follows.

Capitulation—The Ultimate Bear Market Low Indicator

Throughout the history of the stock market there have been innumerable attempts to determine when bear markets are ending and new bull markets are about to begin. It is always difficult to predict when *any* existing trend will change, since one of the laws of physics is that a body in motion tends to stay in motion in the same direction. The difficulty is compounded in the stock market by the need to overcome the negativity and despair that is often found during bear markets. The rewards of being correct can be substantial; however, as the advance from the lows into the first several months of a new bull market is usually the strongest of the entire bull market that follows. I will discuss and compare the eight best indicators that attempt to identify Bear market bottoms and indeed, have identified half of the bear market bottoms during the period of their existence. You will see that none of the others has proven to be as accurate as my Capitulation Indicator which has identified eight of the last twelve market bottoms.

Before we compare any indicator's ability to spot a bear market bottom, hence the beginning of a new bull market, we must have a clear definition for both. Bear market definitions vary from "a nine percent drop (if followed by a recession)" according to *Money Magazine* (10/98), to "a long downward movement interrupted by important rallies" from *The Dow Theory*, and some sources require as much as a 30% drop in the indices to qualify as a bear market, but a 20% drop is most frequently used. *My definition of a bear market is a drop of 16% on both the Dow Jones Industrial Average and the Standard & Poor's 500 Index.* The threshold of minus 16% has resulted in declines of at least 24% nearly 80% of the time. In addition, 16% drops have been followed by a recession over 70% of the time, but requiring a 20% decline has resulted in missing the recessions of 1923–4, 1957–8 and 1980, which were signaled by the 16% definition. It just so happens that a 16% drop is the reciprocal of a 19% rise (it takes a

19% gain to make up for a 16% loss), which is *my definition of a bull market (a 19% rise in both the Dow Jones Industrials and the S&P 500 indices)*. When reaching the 19% threshold the market has continued to advance above 29%, 95% of the time! More than half of these markets rose over 75%, with the average gain posting 115% with a duration of nearly three years (excluding the aberrations of the 1930s). 100% of the bull markets of the 20th and 21st centuries have been accompanied by, or followed shortly thereafter by, economic expansions.

A brief explanation of the eight best indicators for identifying bear market lows follows.

The Equity-Only Put/Call Ratio (the volume of puts traded divided by the volume of calls) is a contrary indicator. To paraphrase Paul Cherney, Chief Market Analyst at Standard & Poor's, "Put/Call ratios are used to quantify extremes in sentiment. The higher number of puts traded versus calls, the greater the possibility that the stock market is at or near the bottom" (*Special Studies*, 8/24/98, S&P Marketscope). Early attempts to identify market bottoms were based on a .75 ratio which was negated as the ETFs (exchange traded funds) such as DIA, SPY and QQQQ were added. However, back-testing this method using a ratio of 1.0 or higher, using the first day, if there are multiple days, when such a signal has occurred at least a month after a previous occurrence, has resulted in the record shown in the Appendix to this report, as are the records of the other indicators to follow. This ratio can be determined from data available at www.cboe.com. It *identified four bear market lows, missed one, and had one extraneous but NO false signals.* An extraneous signal, which occurs in an *existing bull* market, may have its place, but not in this study whose purpose is to identify *bear* market lows and the turn to a new bull market. False signals occur in bear markets but not at or near the lows.

Net Cash Into/Out of Equity Funds is another contrary indicator whereas investors pour money into equity mutual funds when they are optimistic and pull funds out when they are bearish. The Investment Company Institute (www.ici.org) and TrimTabs (www.trimtabs.com) report these numbers shortly after each month-end. When the net withdrawal of funds spikes downward during a reported month and then turns up the following month, delineating the spike, a signal is generating. The problem is in defining a spike and deciding which day or week it could be identified which makes this indicator rather subjective. It *identified the last five bear market lows, missed five, and had three extraneous and two false signals*.

New 52-Week Lows as a Percentage of Issues Traded has been available since January 1978 when the NYSE began calculating new lows (of individual issues) on a trailing 52-week basis. The data is available daily in the *Wall Street Journal* and elsewhere. Paul Cherney of S&P MarketScope describes the "surge in new lows means that people have been dumping stocks at virtually any price. It indicates that the markets are in the throes of a capitulation, but the capitulation might not have seen its low close yet" (*Special Studies*, 10/18/99). This signal is generated using the second day, to eliminate one day wonders, when the percentage move is greater than 15%, and has not occurred within a month of a previous such move. The back-tested results of this indicator has *identified six bear market lows, missed two, and had two extraneous and two false signals*.

The CBOE Volatility Index (VIX) is described by the Chicago Board Options Exchange, where its data is posted (www.cboe.com), as being the benchmark for stock market volatility. It measures investors' expectations of near term volatility based on the prices of stock index options. Presently, it uses out-of-the-money put and call options on the S&P 500 Index with a constant maturity of 30 days to expiration. A level of 42 is the number that has identified the lows since 1998. Unfortunately this Index was only started in 1993 and then revised in 2003 with back-testing only to 1990. Because its record is so brief and totally a result of hindsight, it is unfair to rate it above the others with longer-term records. This indicator *identified three bear market lows, missed one, and had NO extraneous or false signals*.

Lowry's Reports "90%" Indicator won the "Charles H. Dow Award" for Paul Desmond in 2002, available at www.lowrysreports .com or at www.mta.org. In order to generate a signal, several criteria must be met: Downside Volume must equal at least 90% of the total of Upside Volume plus Downside Volume; Points Lost must be at least 90% of the sum of Points Gained and Points Lost; followed in fairly short order by one 90% Upside Day, or two 80% Upside Days. There is some ambiguity in the

90% Indicator in that the usual magic number signaling the end of a bear market is 90, but can also be 80. Since 1960 this Indicator correctly **identified nine bear market bottoms and missed three.** Unfortunately over that same time period it created **sixteen extraneous signals and three false signals.** The record shown in the Appendix has used two or more days of downside to precede a signal, since when one day was used considerably more extraneous and false signals were generated.

The Arms Index developed in 1967 by Richard Arms Jr. of the ARMS Advisory, also known as TRIN, an acronym for Trading Index, is generally considered to be primarily a short-term trading tool. It is determined by dividing the Advance/Decline ratio by the Upside/Downside volume ratio. It can be found daily in the *Wall Street Journal.* If there was 1 advancing stock for each 3 declining stocks (1/3 = .33), and if upside volume was outnumbered by declining volume by 10 time (1/10 + .10) the resultant Index level would be 3.3 (.33/.10). A number of 3 or higher has **identified six bear market bottoms, missed four, and had thirteen extraneous signals and six false signals.**

The 200-Day Moving Average is used by many investors to determine the trend and direction of the market. It is most dependable, however, when the Dow Jones and the S&P 500 are each 20% below their respective 200-day moving averages. My thanks to Paul Cherney of S&P MarketScope for running the numbers for me so I was able to construct the historic record. Numerous Internet chart services such as www.bigcharts.com or www.stockcharts.com show the 200-Day moving average. When both the Dow Jones Industrials and the S&P 500 have descended to such extreme low levels the market has been at or near **six bear market bottom, six bottoms were missed but there were no extraneous or false signals.**

When the percent of NYSE stocks trading above their **10-Week Moving Averages** drops to 10% it can be another indication of market bottoms. I mention it because I believe it may have promise but do not include it because the past data that I have been able to obtain have not indicated exact days, or even exact months. In addition the charts have been revised recently thus making continuity impossible. It is worth watching at www.InvestorsIntelligence.com, but since I cannot vouch for its record I cannot recommend it along with the others.

The following is the most successful of any of the indicators that I am aware of that have a capability for determining when a bear market is ending and a new bull market beginning:

My Capitulation Indicator identifies the capitulation that often accompanies bear market bottoms. Capitulation as it relates to the stock market occurs when investors and/or speculators abandon equities because they are so disheartened, fearful, need to meet margin calls, or for whatever reason sell en masse. This is often called a selling climax as stocks cascade down into a cataclysmic sell-off. Charles Dow or any of his successors in writings about Dow's theory did not utter the word capitulation, but it was clearly alluded to in the early 20th century. Robert Rhea described the third and final phase of a bear market in *The Dow Theory* in 1932 as "caused by distress selling of sound securities, regardless of their value, by those who must find a cash market for at least a portion of their assets." Rhea also wrote, "After a market has drastically declined . . . and then goes into a semi-panic collapse, it is wise to cover short positions **and even perhaps *make commitments for long account*** (*The Dow Theory,* p. 55).

The calculations that I use to identify these capitulations were developed in the mid-1960's by the COMPARE (Computer Assistance to Research) Department at Dean Witter & Co. and the data was first published in 1969. A short-term oscillator is utilized which measures the percent of divergence between the three major stock market indices (Dow Jones Industrial Average, S&P 500 and the New York Stock Exchange Composite) and their ten-week, time-weighted moving averages. Several chart services such as www.profit.net show a similar exponentially smoothed 50-day moving average (EMA). EMAs reduce the lag by applying more weight to recent prices relative to older prices. An explanation of EMAs can be found in numerous texts and websites such as www.stockcharts.com/education/Indicator Analysis. Market bottoms are identified when the divergence between the three major stock market indices is 10% below their respective ten-week, exponentially time-weighted moving averages, and has only been signaled eleven times in the last 50 years. The date used is the first day the level was attained. My database covers back to 1953 and I have personally calculated and maintained the database for many years since Dean Witter, now

Morgan Stanley, long ago abandoned the Department respon-
sible for its updating. This Indicator has *identified eight of the
last twelve bear market bottoms, including the last five market bottoms on a real time basis! It had no signal at four other
bottoms—some bear markets end with a whimper—and has
never generated a false or extraneous signal.*

Its signals were *the best of all eight indicators* at seven of the ten
bottoms that were identified by any of the indicators, as you will
see in Exhibit 1 [Table 8.2]. It came in second-best one time when
its signal was one day early! A critical advantage over the other
indicators is that the market levels that would cause the threshold of capitulation to be reached can be, and has been, calculated and communicated during the week *prior* to its happening
so that investors can get a heads-up ahead of time.

In summary, all the indicators have identified at least half of
the market bottoms during the period of their existence, at or
near the time they were entering new bull markets. Of the last
twelve bear market bottoms, only 1978 and 1982 were not identified by one or more of these indicators. Lowry's and my Capitulation Indicator captured 2/3rds of those markets lows over the
last 43 years. The following chart shows a large "X" indicating
which signal(s) was *closest in market level to the actual low point of
the bear market.* A small "x" indicates that a signal was also given,
but was not the closest. The record clearly indicates that bear
market bottoms CAN be identified by one or more methods,
even 8 different ways, as was the case for 2002.

With definitions and explanations in place, the results are
shown [in Table 8.2].

So how does it work out in the stock market? [Table 8.3]
shows the result for the S&P 500 three months, six months, nine
months and a year after the Capitulation Signal with the average
gains being +11%, +18.5%, +24.7% and 25.4% respectively.

The 11 dates listed in Table 8.3 are the only times capitulation has been attained on my indicator (see Figure 8.9).

Robert Rhea wrote "Hamilton tells us not to try to use the
Dow Theory to pick the day when the lows of a bear market are
to be made: 'No knowledge of the stock market barometer will
enable any of us to call the absolute turn from a bear market to a
bull market'" (*The Dow Theory*, p. 40). That was certainly the case
in the first part of the 20th century, but it HAS been possible

Table 8.2 Exhibit 1

Bear Low	Capitulation	Lowry's	Arms	Lows/Total	200Day	Inflow/Out	VIX	Put/Call
1962	X	x	n/a	n/a	x	n/a	n/a	n/a
1966	no signal	X	n/a	n/a	no signal	n/a	n/a	n/a
1970	x*	x	x	n/a	X	no signal	n/a	n/a
1974	X	x	x	n/a	x	no signal	n/a	n/a
1978	no signal	no signal	no signal	no signal	no signal	no signal	n/a	n/a
1980	no signal	x	X	x	no signal	no signal	n/a	n/a
1982	no signal	no signal	no signal	no signal	no signal	no signal	n/a	n/a
1987	X	x	X	X	X	x	n/a	x
1990	X	x	no signal	x	no signal	x	no signal	no signal
1998	X	x	X	x	X	x	X	x
2001	X	no signal	no signal	x	x	x	X	x
2002	X	x—in 2003	x	x*	x	x	x	x
# Identified†	8	9	6	6	6	5	3	4
# times BEST	7	1	3	1	3	0	2	0
# Missed	4	4	4	2	6	5	1	1
# Extraneous(‡)	0	16	13	2	0	3	0	1
# False ($)	0	3	6	2	0	2	0	0

n/a = Indicator or data not available.

*Missed the low by one day. Actually, Lowry's 2002 low signal was in March of 2003 but was within 10% of the low.

†Signaled low within 2 months and/or 10% of the low point.

‡Signaled in already existing bull market, may have been useful but not for picking the bottom.

§Signaled during bear market but more than 3 months premature to the bottom.

Table 8.3 Exhibit 2: My Capitulation Buy Signals and the S&P 500 Gain Thereafter (Data since December 31, 1953)

BUY	Date	Level	3 Months		6 Months		9 Months		1 Year	
			Level	Gain	Level	Gain	Level	Gain	Level	Gain
1.	6/22/1962	52.68	57.69	9.5%	62.64	18.9%	66.19	25.6%	70.25	33.4%
2.	5/25/1970	70.25	81.12	15.5%	85.09	21.1%	96.92	38.0%	99.47	41.6%
3.	8/23/1974	71.55	68.9	-3.7%	82.62	15.5%	90.58	26.6%	84.28	17.8%
4.	9/30/1974	63.54	67.16	5.7%	83.85	32.0%	95.19	49.8%	83.87	32.0%
5.	10/19/1987	224.84	249.32	10.9%	257.92	14.7%	268.47	19.4%	276.97	23.2%
6.	12/3/1987	225.21	267.88	18.9%	266.45	18.3%	264.48	17.4%	271.81	20.7%
7.	8/23/1990	307.06	315.1	2.6%	365.65	19.1%	374.96	22.1%	394.17	28.4%
8.	8/31/1998	957.28	1163.63	21.6%	1238.33	29.4%	1301.84	36.0%	1320.41	37.9%
9.	9/20/2001*	984.54	1139.93	15.8%	1151.85	17.0%	1006.29	2.2%	920.47	-6.5%
10.	7/19/2002	847.76	884.39	4.3%	901.78	6.4%	893.58	5.4%	993.32	17.2%
11.	10/9/2002	776.76	927.58	19.4%	865.99	11.5%	1002.21	29.0%	1038.73	33.7%
Average				**11.0%**		**18.5%**		**24.7%**		**25.4%**

*This shortest bull market, which began 9/21/01, rose just +21% for the S&P 500 (+29% on the Dow) and lasted only 6 months to 3/19/02 and then reverted to an "official" bear market (down −16% on both the Dow Industrials *and* the S&P 500) on 7/10/02 at the level shown under "1 Year."

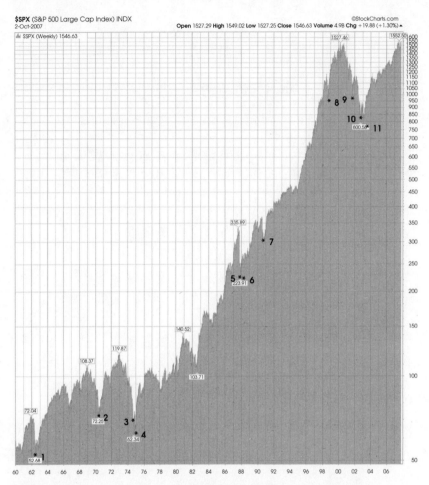

Figure 8.9 11 Times that Capitulation Has Been Attained by My Indicator

since the latter part of that century. There is a ***definite and measurable level of capitulation*** that comes in at or near market lows. Of the **eleven** times that capitulation has met the defined levels in my database, **three** have been *on THE day of the bear market low,* **five** others have been *one to three days before* the lows and within 2% of the lows. The average of the eleven was within 3.2% of the low close on the Dow Jones Industrials and/or the S&P 500, as can be calculated from the data found in Exhibit Two and the APPENDIX. I have no doubt that Charles Dow would have welcomed the discovery of such a way to clearly identify the "semi-panic collapse" he observed, in order to "make commitments for long account."

Respectfully Submitted by Jack Schannep

Author's note: The specific details of the comparisons for all eight indicators are shown in Appendix B.

Now that we have an understanding of how important, and at the same time normal, capitulation is, we should look forward to its occurrence at the end of bear markets. With this capability to identify and take advantage of capitulation, we next explore how to incorporate it into improving the Dow Theory for the twenty-first century.

The Heart of the Theory

N ow we have the ingredients from prior chapters to put together a way to improve the timeliness of the Dow Theory as an indicator of when to buy and when to sell. With a firm understanding of the original Dow Theory, a logical definition of bull and bear, and the ability to use capitulation to our advantage, we can formulate a Dow Theory for the twenty-first century that should help us invest more successfully.

The Dow Jones Industrials and the Standard & Poor's 500

In 1957, the Standard & Poor's Corporation combined previous indices that it had maintained since 1923 into the Standard & Poor's 500 Stock Price Index. Usually referred to as the S&P 500, the index has had a parallel result with the Dow Jones Industrials in tracking the stock market over the last 50 years. Both have had an incredibly similar performance; seldom are they more than 10 percent apart on an annual basis. For the 10 years ending December 31, 1999, the increase for the Dow Jones was 317.6 percent versus 315.4 percent for the S&P 500 (*less than a* 1 percent *difference over 10 years*). In the decade of the 1980s, the difference was even smaller: 228.3 percent for the Dow and 227.4 percent for the S&P. *More than half of the time* (56 percent since the S&P 500 was backtested to 1949), the bull market tops *and* bear market bottoms of both indices have been on *the same day*.

For all intents and purposes, they are the same . . . or are they? At last look, the total global capitalization on the New York Stock Exchange (NYSE) was about 5.3 times that of the Nasdaq. Therefore, a properly balanced *total market indicator* should include **84 percent** NYSE and **16 percent** Nasdaq. Since the Dow Jones Industrial Average (DJIA) actually includes 2 Nasdaq stocks, the 28 from the NYSE gives it a **93** percent representation. The S&P 500 contains 75 Nasdaq stocks, but its 425 from the NYSE gives it an **85 percent** representation there. Because the S&P 500 is closest to the "proper" mix, it would seem that, *on that basis* it should be used instead of the Dow Jones Industrials.

The Dow Jones Industrials do contain 20 of the 50 largest U.S. companies, but it does not include the other 30. The S&P 500 includes 91 of the largest 100 companies. The 30-stock Dow Jones Industrials are impacted disproportionately by the movement of just 8 companies, which are weighted between 4 and 6 percent of that index; no single stock exerts that much influence on the S&P 500. These are some of the reasons most professional investors use the S&P 500 index as a benchmark rather than the DJIA. There is 10 times the amount of money invested in the exchange-traded funds in "Spiders" that track the S&P 500 than the "Diamonds" that track the Dow Jones Industrials.

I have backtested the results of using the S&P 500 from its origin in 1957 in comparison with the DJIA for use in the Dow Theory. I found that it and the Dow Jones Industrials alternate between working better than each other during different time frames. That does not mean you should stick with *one or the other*; it means **you should include them *both* in determining Dow Theory signals**. Charles Dow only had his two indices, the Industrial and the Rails, to use in his formulation of the Dow Theory, but since 1957, when the S&P 500 came into existence, there has been the option to use it in conjunction with the original two in determining signals.

The Dow Jones Transports

My first inclination was to consider the S&P 500 as an alternative to the Dow Jones Transports, as many people think the Transports are from a different era. However, FedEx, UPS, the truckers, airlines, and yes, even the railroads are essential to business in the twenty-first century. But I did find an improvement to the record of the

Dow Theory with the substitution of the S&P 500 for the Transports. In fact, a *quarter* of the 41 signals over the last 47 years would have been improved.

I then looked at what the results of using two of the three indices confirming one another would have been. Using the Dow Jones Industrials, Transports, and the S&P 500 Index with *any* two of the three indices confirming one another, as per the original Dow Theory, showed really exciting results. More than *two-thirds* of the signals were improved on significantly, nearly 2 percent better per signal. When I added up the participation of each of the Industrials, Transports, and S&P 500, I found that nearly all the signals involved the S&P 500 with confirmation coming from either the Industrials and/or the Transports. That is when it became obvious that *the Standard & Poor's 500 is the preeminent index in interpreting the Dow Theory in the twenty-first century.*

Whenever either the Industrials or Transports confirm the S&P 500, then *a signal is given.* Over the last 48 years, there have been 44 signals given with the Dow Jones Industrials confirming 30 of them and the Transports confirming 20 signals (sometimes both confirmed on the same day). The S&P 500 has been a part of 42 signals. Only twice did the Industrials and Transports combine for signals ahead of the S&P 500. **When such an original Dow Theory signal occurs, it should be followed. In other words, *the first to give a signal is the winner*!** And, of course, I am adding capitulation, when it occurs, as the time to start buying into the Dow Theory, and that brings the results up to nearly *three-quarters* of the old signals being improved on. Actually two signals were sooner but 0.1 and 1.1 percent poorer prices, and one new sell signal followed by a rebuy signal lost 1.5 percent. Still, the improvement *on average for all 44 Dow Theory signals since 1957 was over 2* percent *per signal.*

After that horrendous day on September 11, 2001, my interpretation of the traditional Dow Theory got a buy signal on 11/8 at the **9587.52** level. The market had a mini–bull market that only lasted six months but did rise 29 percent. After that top, it headed back into a continuing bear market that would take it to new lows in 2002. Table 9.1 shows how using the S&P 500 with the Dow Industrials and Transports helped give a profitable sell signal rather than the losing signal the traditional Dow Theory would have given. After the March highs, a pullback occurred that met the requirements of a secondary reaction. Then a bounce came that

Table 9.1   S&P 500 Impact on a Dow Theory Sell Signal

Date	DJ Ind	%	Status	Date	Transp	%	Date	S&P	%
3/19/02	10635.25		Bull High	3/4	3049.96		3/19	1170.29	
5/6	**9808.04**	−7.8	Pullback	5/10	**2643.10**	−3.3	5/7	**1049.49**	−10.3
5/18	10353.08	+5.6	Bounce	5/17	2798.36	+5.9	5/17	1106.59	+5.4
6/3	**9709.79<**		Break/BUY	6/3	2689.83		**6/3**	**1040.68<**	
6/25	**9126.80**		BUY	**6/25**	2627.92<				

failed to reach the earlier highs; a classic S-1 signal was thus shaping up. The Industrials and the S&P 500 then rolled over and fell through their previous pullback lows on June 3, 2002, giving a sell signal under the rules of the Dow Theory for the twenty-first century. Unfortunately, the Transports were still above their pullback lows on that date; they did drop through three weeks later to confirm a traditional Dow Theory sell. The difference of the first sell at **9709.79**, which was a small profit from the previous buy at 9587.52, and the late sell at **9126.92** was, of course, 582.87, an amount that did not need to have been lost.

An Aggressive Yet Prudent Approach

Of the last half dozen traditional Dow Theory buy signals, the improvement using the approach proposed in this chapter would have averaged a 5.7 percent lower/better entry level than the original Dow Theory. Five of the six were at better entry levels and one was not; it was 0.04 percent higher.

A Dow Theory buy signal has *always* followed "capitulation" since 1953 when my database began; therefore, I have incorporated it into my twenty-first-century adaptation. **I would suggest buying an initial 25 percent of your intended investment position at capitulation. If there is a second capitulation (as has occurred three times over the last 50 years), then add another 25 percent at that time.** Starting to buy ahead of a forthcoming Dow Theory buy signal at or near the lows will of course lower the average entry level into the stock market. This makes obsolete the criticism that the Dow Theory buys are too late.

After capitulations, there is typically a bounce of 5 to 15 percent followed by a setback of 3 to 10 percent or so on one or the other of the Industrial, Transport, or S&P 500 averages. *Since it is a requirement for a Dow Theory buy signal* that one or the other of the indices pulls back at least 3 percent, investors would be wise to **add another 25 percent to their holdings on the occasion of that pullback**.

On the rare occasion when a bull market is reached *by definition* (up 19 percent on both the Dow Jones Industrials and the S&P 500), prior to a Dow Theory buy signal being completed, a further 25 percent should be added. We know that after attaining my definition of being a bull market, a bull market typically has much further to rise, as you have seen in Chapter 5. I have no doubt Mr. Dow would like his theory to be engaged in that rise. If a completed Dow Theory buy signal and new bull market were not to follow some future capitulation, then you would be partially invested in what would be a failed upturn. In that case, if the markets then were to go on to new lows on two of the three indices, selling out of the position would be indicated into that continuing bear market. But this has not happened over the last 50 years.

You should then **complete your full 100 percent position when the new Dow Theory buy signal is finalized**. The final buy would be in accordance with the original interpretation but using the first two of the three indices rising above the initial bounce.

Improvements Add to the Profit to Your Investment Portfolio

The enhancements to the Dow Theory results over the last 47 years using capitulation, buying after the pullback, and the confirmation of two of the three of the Dow Jones Industrials, Dow Jones Transports, and the S&P 500 Index to give a signal would have resulted in a betterment to 32 signals out of the total 44. That added value to fully 72 percent of those signals would have made a tremendous difference in improving the already outstanding results of the Dow Theory. The average improvement was 2.2 percent for each of the 44 signals, which of course includes all buys and sells. Since there was nearly one signal a year, actually one each 13 months on average, that equates to *an extra 2-plus percent per year* over the 47-year period.

It has been said that due to my improvements, this is not Dow Theory, it is Schannep theory. I don't think one wants to fly a jet aircraft without an altimeter, compass, or fuel gauge just because the Wright brothers flew that way in 1907. I appreciate Mr. Dow and the Wright brothers for what they started, but the world has come a long way from the start of the twentieth century. I suggest we take advantages of the advances we've seen over that time. In *The Dow Theory*, Robert Rhea wrote that "the usefulness of the Dow Theory improves with age. Certainly a more comprehensive study of the subject is possible with a 35-year record before us than when Dow worked with the figures of only a few years, while *those who use it 20 years from now will have a greater advantage* than we now enjoy." It has been over 75 years since he wrote those words, 75 years in which we have seen a great depression, 17 bull and bear markets, wars, good times, bad times, and the unbelievable events of Pearl Harbor and 9/11. And through it all the old reliable Dow Theory has prevailed, even in its most basic interpretation. Is it too much to think we might add value to the theory in the twenty-first century?

Let's use the first capitulation as an example of how and when to buy. It will also serve as an example of the advantage of starting to invest at the time of a capitulation. This example is laid out in Table 9.2. **Buy the first 25 percent at the time of the capitulation** on June 22, 1962 at **539.19**. Since the levels at which capitulation occurs can be determined ahead of time, it makes it possible to buy at the close on *that* day. From the lows that week on June 25 and 26, the market bounced over the next two to three weeks with the Dow

Table 9.2   Buy Signal Following Capitulation

Date	Industrials	%	Status	Date	Transport	%	Date	S&P	%
6/22/62	**539.19**		**Capitulation**						
6/26	535.76		Bear market low	6/25	115.89		6/26	52.32	
7/12	590.27<	+10.2	Bounce	7/16	125.49<	+8.3	7/12	**58.03<**	+10.9
7/18	571.24	−3.2	*Pullback*	8/13	119.28	−4.9	7/18	56.20	−3.2
7/30	**591.44<**		*Break up/* Not	8/27	125.16		7/31	**58.23<**	
7/31	**597.93**		*Buy*						
8/23	616.00		Higher				8/22	59.78	
10/23	558.06		Low/*Bear low*	10/1	**114.86**	−8.5	10/23	53.49	
11/9	**616.13**		Traditional buy	11/9	126.05<			60.16	

Industrials rising 10.2 percent to 590.27 on July 12. A 3 percent pullback then occurred on July 18 with a drop to **571.24.** That is also when the S&P 500 had its first 3 percent pullback.

When the first index completes a 3 percent pullback, add another 25 percent position to bring the invested portion to 50 percent. The Transports topped out on July 16 and took until July 25 to reach a 3 percent pullback. After a 4.9 percent drop, they bounced up but failed to exceed their first bounce top. They then fell to a new bear market low on October 1, for a total 8.5 percent pullback.

The Transports rose to a belated buy on November 9. That was the date of the "traditional" Dow Theory buy signal. The *newer* interpretation of the Dow Theory had long since had a buy signal when the S&P 500 joined the Industrials in exceeding their bounce highs on July 31 at **597.93,** at which time the final 50 percent was invested for an *average entry level* of **576.59,** *some 6.4* percent *lower than the traditional buy at 616.13.* The average entry level of all buy signals *related to capitulation* was 5.3 percent lower (better) than the traditional Dow Theory buy level.

The time frame for the bounce was several days short of the *usual* "three weeks to as many months" for a *secondary* reaction. This is of no concern because Hamilton had said it could even be from "a few *days* to many weeks" and the market was actually changing to a new *primary* trend. The pullback lasted less than a week. After a capitulation, things happen faster than is usually the case at tops. Therefore, after capitulation, I would eliminate any time requirement whatsoever for the presumed secondary reaction in determining a buy signal, which, it turns out, is the new primary trend. When capitulation is absent, I would shorten to about a two-week minimum time frame the definition of a secondary reaction, rather than the old "three weeks to as many months" requirement. This actually conforms with Charles Dow's *initial* definition: "The second is the short swing, running from *two weeks* to a month or more."

Only after a capitulation would I preempt the Dow Theory buy to the extent of an entry during the pullback phase. We know that Dow Theory buy signals have always followed capitulation, but *other* potential buy signal setups without capitulation do not always pan out, *so don't anticipate them.* Let the finalized buy signal be your entry point in those other cases.

There is a phenomenon called "the bouncing ball" where a ball bounces sharply from the bottom but rolls over at the top. Similarly,

Table 9.3 Capitulation and Subsequent Buy Levels

	Capitulation		Bear Market Low		Bounce		Pullback		1st −3%*	Dow Theory Buy		Average Entry	Lower than Original Buy
Date	Date	Level	Date	Level	High Pt	%	Low Pt	−%	Level	Date	Level		
		Buy 25% each time							Buy 25%		Buy to 100%		
6/22/1962	6/22/1962	539.19	6/26/1962	535.76	590.27	10.20%	571.24	−3.20%	571.24	7/31/1962	597.93	576.57	−6.4%
5/25/1970	5/25/1970	641.36	5/26/1970	631.16	720.43	14.10%	669.36	−7.10% *ind/S&P on July 18	694.35	8/21/1970	745.41	706.63	−6.9%
8/23/1974	8/23/1974	686.80	10/4/1974	584.56	673.50	15.20%	633.84	−5.90% *S&P on June 10	658.17	11/1/1974	665.28	654.53	−3.0%
9/30/1974	9/30/1974	607.87	10/4/1974	584.56	673.50	15.20%	633.84	−5.90% *S&P on Sept. 10	658.17	11/1/1974	665.28		
10/19/1987	10/19/1987	1738.74	10/19/1987	1738.74	2027.85	16.60%	1793.93	−11.50%	1950.43	1/7/1988	2031.50	1874.30	−8.7%
12/3/1987	12/3/1987	1776.53	10/19/1987	1738.74	2027.85	16.60%	1793.93	−11.50% *all on Oct. 22	1950.43	1/7/1988	2031.50		
8/23/1990	8/23/1990	2483.42	10/11/1990	2365.10	2520.79	6.60%	2430.20	−3.60% *all on Sept. 20	2518.32	11/12/1990	2540.35	2520.61	−3.4%
8/31/1998	8/31/1998	7539.07	8/31/1998	7539.07	8020.78	6.40%	7615.54	−5.10% *all on Sept. 10	7615.54	9/14/1998	7945.35	7761.33	−3.3%

9/20/2001	**8376.21**	9/21/2001	8235.81	15.90%	9075.14	−4.90%	**9344.16**	11/6/2001
							*trans on Oct. 12	
7/19/2002	**8019.26**	7/23/2002	7702.34	13.40%	8043.63	−7.90%	**8506.62**	8/14/2002
							*trans on Aug. 1	
10/9/2002	**7286.27**	10/9/2002	7286.27	17.20%	8538.24	−2.60%	**8368.94**	11/4/2002
							*trans on Oct. 29	

9591.12	9225.65	−3.8%	
8743.31	8503.13	−5.1%	
8571.60	8061.52	−7.1%	

Average Bounce	+**12.8%**	Average Pullback	−**5.8%**
		Average Lower Entry	−**5.3%**

*First index to pullback 3% is listed along with the date of pullback.

Author's note: The underlined capitulation level is the second capitulation when another 25 percent is added. For instance, the November 4, 2002 signal includes 1/4 purchase at each of 7/19, 10/9, 10/29, and 11/4.

the stock market tends to bounce up sharply and quickly at bottoms, but takes longer to "top out" at market tops. Nonetheless, I would still use the same "to about a two-week minimum time frame" for secondary reactions at tops, even though they may actually take longer than at bottoms. There are more signals using the compressed time frame requirements for secondary reactions than with the original "requirements/suggestions." Not all are profitable, but overall the results are greatly enhanced.

In Table 9.3, I have used the 3 percent pullback after the initial bounce to add to the position taken at the time of capitulation. I have determined the date at which that dip was actually first attained by any *one of* the Industrials, Transports, or the S&P 500, and used that as the prevailing market level. This *is* the minimum pullback, and it would be tempting to wait for a further pullback, but there is no way of knowing what the extent of the pullback will be, only that the 3 percent figure qualifies for a potential Dow Theory buy signal. The final percentage, usually 50 percent, is added at the new Dow Theory buy signal. The results are shown in Table 9.4.

Sell signals have invariably resulted in the market going lower an average of 14.6 percent over the ensuing months As can be seen from Table 9.5, the actual results cover a wide range of percentage losses, as well as a wide range for the time frame for those losses. In Chapter 15 you will see that this indicator has the best record for selling with the greatest loss to follow.

Detailed Record of the New Dow Theory for the Twenty-First Century

Table 9.6 shows a tabulation of the signals that would have been given over the last 50 years using the recommendations in this chapter. On the left is the type signal. The center shows the bounces, pullbacks, and other parts of the Dow Theory signals for the Dow Jones Industrials and Transports as well as the S&P 500 Index. On the right is the improvement added by including the S&P 500 over relying on just the Industrials and Transports. If you follow through a few of these signals, you will better understand how they were arrived at. I have not included a graph of this record as I did for the traditional Dow Theory shown in Chapter 3, as the improvements do not show up significantly in graphic form. Each signal's

Table 9.4 Results after "New" Buy Signals (data since October 22, 1957)

Date	Level	3 Months Level	Gain	6 Months Level	Gain	9 Months Level	Gain	1 year Level	Gain	To Sell Signal Sell Date	Level	Gain	Months
11/29/1957	41.72	40.84	-2.1%	44.09	5.7%	47.75	14.5%	52.48	25.8%	2/16/1960	54.73	31.2%	26.5
5/16/1961	67.08	67.73	1.0%	71.62	6.8%	70.59	5.2%	67.71	0.9%*	4/12/1962	67.71	0.9%	10.9
7/31/1962	56.34	56.52	0.3%	66.20	17.5%	69.80	23.9%	69.13	22.7%	5/5/1966	87.93	56.1%	45.2
12/13/1966	82.73	88.43	6.9%	92.62	12.0%	95.99	16.0%	94.42	14.1%*	10/24/1967	94.42	14.1%	11.3
9/24/1968	102.59	105.04	2.4%	99.79	-2.7%*					2/20/1969	99.79	-2.7%	4.9
10/16/1969	96.37	90.92	-5.7%	88.17	-8.5%*					1/26/1970	88.17	-8.5%	3.3
8/21/1970	76.05	83.72	10.1%	96.74	27.2%	100.99	32.8%	97.07	27.6%*	7/28/1971	97.07	27.6%	11.2
1/12/1972	103.59	110.18	6.4%	106.89	3.2%	108.80	5.0%	119.30	15.2%	3/21/1973	110.49	6.7%	14.3
11/1/1974	69.55	76.98	10.7%	88.10	26.7%	87.99	26.5%	89.04	28.0%	3/30/1977	98.54	41.7%	28.9
6/5/1978	99.95	104.49	4.5%	101.26	1.3%*					10/17/1978	101.26	1.3%	5.4
1/4/1979	98.58	102.65	4.1%	102.09	3.6%	110.17	11.8%	106.52	8.1%	7/2/1981	128.64	30.5%	29.9
10/6/1982	125.97	145.27	15.3%	151.04	19.9%	168.48	33.7%	170.28	35.2%	1/24/1984	165.94	31.7%	15.6
11/6/1984	170.41	180.43	5.9%	179.99	5.6%	187.93	10.3%	192.76	13.1%	10/14/1987	305.23	79.1%	35.3
1/5/1988	239.23	258.51	8.1%	275.81	15.3%	271.86	13.6%	280.01	17.0%	10/13/1989	333.62	39.5%	21.3
5/11/1990	352.00	351.48	-0.1%*	351.48	-0.1%					8/2/1990	351.48	-0.1%	2.7
11/12/1990	314.38	365.50	16.3%	375.74	19.5%	388.02	23.4%	396.74	26.2%	8/4/1998	1072.1	241.0%	92.7
9/14/1998	999.23	1141.20	14.2%	1294.6	29.6%	1294.00	29.5%	1336.3	33.7%	8/10/1999	1281.4	28.2%	10.9
11/6/2001	1078.5	1083.50	0.5%	1052.7	-2.4%	1040.68	-3.5%*			6/3/2002	1040.7	-3.5%	6.9
8/14/2002	892.91	873.52	-2.2%	873.52	1.3%*					9/17/2002	873.52	-2.2%	1.1
11/4/2002	868.90	861.40	-0.9%	861.40	1.6%*					1/24/2003	861.4	-0.9%	2.7
4/22/2003	911.37	988.11	8.4%	1030.4	13.1%	1143.94	25.5%	1139.9	25.1%	5/10/2004	1097.1	20.4%	12.6
11/3/2004	1143.20	1189.89	4.1%	1161.2	1.6%	1245.04	8.9%	1219.9	6.7%				
Average:			**4.7%**		**10.2%**		**16.8%**		**19.5%**			**30.1%**	**18.7**

Average Annual Gain Buy to Sell including dividends: **20.5%**

*Ends at Dow Theory sell signals

Author's note: Average is for all that completed or were closed out by sell signals in that period.

Table 9.5   Dow Theory for the Twenty-First Century Sell Signals and the Further S&P 500 Loss to the Final Bear Market Lows (data since October 22, 1957)

Sell Date	Level	Low Date	Level	Further Loss	Months to Low
2/16/1960	54.73	10/25/1960	52.30*	4.4%	8.3
4/12/1962	67.71	6/26/1962	52.32	22.7%	2.5
5/5/1966	87.93	10/7/1966	73.20	16.8%	5.0
10/24/1967	94.42	3/5/1968	87.72*	7.1%	4.4
2/20/1969	99.79	7/29/1969	89.48*	10.3%	5.3
1/26/1970	88.17	5/26/1970	69.29	21.4%	4.0
7/28/1971	97.07	11/23/1971	90.16	7.1%	4.0
3/21/1973	110.49	10/3/1974	62.28*	43.6%	18.4
3/30/1977	98.54	3/6/1978	86.90	11.8%	4.2
10/17/1978	101.26	11/14/1978	92.49	8.7%	0.9
7/2/1981	128.64	8/12/1982	102.42	20.4%	12.3
1/24/1984	165.94	7/24/1984	147.82*	10.9%	5.1
10/14/1987	305.23	12/4/1987	223.92	26.6%	1.7
10/13/1989	333.62	1/30/1990	322.98*	3.2%	3.6
8/2/1990	351.48	10/11/1990	295.46	15.9%	2.3
8/4/1998	1072.12	8/31/1998	957.28	10.7%	0.9
8/10/1999	1281.43	9/20/2001	965.54	24.7%	24.3
6/3/2002	1040.68	8/5/2002	834.60*	19.8%	2.1
9/17/2002	873.52	10/9/2002	776.76	11.1%	0.8
1/24/2003	861.40	3/11/2003	800.73	7.0%	1.6
5/10/2004	1097.12	8/12/2004	1063.23*	3.1%	2.9
8/14/2007	1426.54				
Average Further Decline: 14.6% over 5.5 months					

*When no "official" bear market follows, this market level is the low for the move. Thirteen signals were followed by "official" bear markets, eight were not.

Table 9.6 Improved Record

Signal-Type (from Chapter 2)	Date:	DJ Ind.	%	Status:	Date:	DJ Trans	%	Date:	S&P 500	%	% Better than Original Dow Theory Signals
	10/22/57	419.79		**Bear Market Low**	10/22	107.21		10/22	38.98		
	10/31/57	441.04	5.1%	Bounce	10/23	113.16	5.5%	10/31	41.06	5.3%	
	11/14/57	427.94	-3.0%	Pullback/**NewLow**	11/19	98.77	-12.7%	11/14	39.44	-3.9%	
	11/22/57	442.88		**Breakup**/Bounce	5/6	113.70		11/29	41.72		
Buy-2	**11/29/57**	**449.87**				(highs)					**2.1%**
	5/2/58	**459.56**		(See Note 1 1.1%)							
	8/3/59	678.10		Market Highs	7/7	173.56		8/3	60.71		
	9/22/59	616.45	-9.1%	Pullback	9/22	150.28	-13.4%	9/22	55.14	-9.2%	
	1/5/60	685.47	11.2%	**New High**/Bounce	10/16	159.99	6.5%	1/5	60.39	9.5%	
Sell-2	**2/16/60**	**611.33**		Breakdown	11/13	149.45		2/16	54.73		**-0.1%**
	3/3/60	**612.05**									
	10/25/60	566.05		Market Lows	9/29	123.37		10/25	52.30		
	4/17/61	696.72	23.1%	Bounce	3/22	150.81	22.2%	4/17	66.68	27.5%	
	4/24/61	672.66	-3.5%	Pullback	4/25	140.04	-7.1%	4/24	64.40	-3.4%	
Buy-1	**5/16/61**	**697.74**		Breakup/Bounce	5/17	148.02		5/15	66.83		**1.3%**
	10/10/61	**706.67**						(5/16)	(67.08)		
	12/13/61	734.91		**Bull Market High**	10/11	152.92		12/12	72.64		
	1/29/62	689.92	-6.1%	Pullback	12/20	140.66	-8.0%	1/29	67.90	-6.5%	
	3/15/61	723.54	4.9%	Bounce	2/2	149.83	6.5%	3/15	71.06	4.7%	
Sell-1	**4/12/62**	**685.67**		Breakdown	4/26	140.28		4/12	67.71		**1.0%**
	4/26/62	**678.68**									
	6/26/62	535.76		**Bear Market Low**	6/25	115.89		6/26	52.32		
	7/12/62	590.27	10.2%	Bounce	7/16	125.49	8.3%	7/12	58.03	10.9%	

(continued)

Table 9.6 (continued)

Signal-Type (from Chapter 2)	Date:	DJ Ind.	%	Status:	Date:	DJ Trans	%	Date:	S&P 500	%	% Better than Original Dow Theory Signals
	7/18/62	571.24	-3.2%	Pullback/**New Low**	10/1	114.86	-8.5%	7/18	56.20	-3.2%	
	7/30/62	591.44		Breakup	11/9	126.05		7/31	58.23		
Buy-2	**7/31/62**	**597.93***									**6.4%**
	11/9/62	**616.13**									
	2/9/66	995.15		***Bull Market High***	2/15	271.72		2/9	94.06		
	3/19/66	911.08	-8.4%	Pullback	3/15	243.60	-10.3%	3/15	87.35	-7.1%	
	4/21/66	954.73	4.8%	Bounce	4/20	265.97	9.2%	4/21	92.42	5.8%	
Sell-1	**5/5/66**	**899.77**		Breakdown	5/5	240.96		5/9	86.32		**0.0%**
	5/5/66	**899.77**						(5/5)	(87.93)		
	10/7/66	744.32		**Bear Market Low**	10/7	184.34		10/7	73.20		
	11/16/66	820.87	10.3%	Bounce	11/16	208.79	13.3%	11/16	82.37	12.5%	
	12/2/66	789.47	-3.8%	Pullback	11/22	199.54	-4.4%	11/22	79.67	-3.3%	
	1/11/67	822.49		Breakup	12/13	208.82		12/12	83.00		
Buy-1	**12/13/66**	**816.70**						(12/13)	82.73)		**0.7%**
	1/11/67	**822.49**									
	8/9/67	926.72		Market Highs	8/4	274.49		8/4	95.83		
	8/30/67	893.72	-3.6%	Pullback	8/22	256.06	-6.7%	8/28	92.64	-3.3%	
	9/25/67	943.08	5.5%	**New High**/Bounce	9/18	265.11	3.5%	9/25	97.59	5.3%	
Sell-2	**10/24/67**	**888.18**		Breakdown	10/10	254.59		11/2	92.34		**0.0%**
	10/24/67	**888.18**						(10/24)	(94.42)		
	3/21/68	825.13		Market Lows	3/5	214.58		3/5	87.72		
	7/15/68	923.72	11.9%	Bounce	7/8	269.61	25.6%	7/11	102.39	16.7%	
	8/9/68	869.65	-5.9%	Pullback	8/9	245.76	-8.8%	8/2	96.63	-5.6%	

*becomes 576.57 & 56.34 buying 1/4 at capitulation, 1/4 on pullback, and final 1/2 at Dow theory buy signal.

Signal	Date	Value	Event	%	Date	Value	%	Date	Value	%	%
	9/9/68	924.98	Breakup		10/1	270.24		9/24	102.59		**0.4%**
Buy-1	**9/24/68**	**938.28**									
	10/1/68	**942.32**									
	12/3/68	985.21	**Bull Market High**		12/1	279.48		11/29	108.37		
	1/8/69	921.25	Pullback	-6.5%	1/13	260.04	-7.0%	1/13	100.40	-7.4%	
	2/13/69	952.70	**Bounce/New high**	3.4%	2/7	279.88	7.6%	2/13	103.71	3.3%	
Sell-2	**2/20/69**	**916.65**	Breakdown		2/25	257.07		2/20	99.79		**1.9%**
	2/25/69	**899.80**									
	7/29/69	801.96	Market Lows		7/30	193.19		7/29	89.48		
	9/2/69	837.78	Bounce	4.5%	8/22	202.02	4.6%	8/22	95.92	7.2%	
	9/8/69	811.84	Pullback	-3.1%	10/9	194.72	-3.6%	9/8	92.70	-3.4%	
Buy-1	**10/16/69**	**838.77**	Breakup		10/27	202.37		10/16	96.37		**2.5%**
	10/27/69	**860.28**									
	11/10/69	863.05	Market Highs		10/28	202.45		11/10	98.33		
	12/17/69	769.93	Pullback	-10.8%	12/16	169.43	-16.3%	12/17	89.20	-9.3%	
	1/5/70	811.31	Bounce	5.4%	1/5	183.31	8.2%	1/5	93.46	4.8%	
Sell-1	**1/26/70**	**768.88**	Breakdown		1/26	168.98		1/23	89.07		**0.0%**
	1/26/70	**768.88**						(1/26	88.17)		
	5/26/70	631.16	**Bear Market Low**		5/26	131.53		5/26	69.29		
	6/19/70	720.43	Bounce	14.1%	6/3	146.98	11.7%	6/3	78.52	13.3%	
	7/7/70	669.36	Pullback/New Low	-7.1%	7/7	116.69	-20.6%	7/7	71.23	-9.3%	
	7/16/70	723.44	Breakup		9/28	148.21		8/21	79.24		
Buy-2	**8/21/70**	**745.41***			8/21	130.60					**6.9%**
	9/28/70	**758.97**									(See Note 2) 6.0%

*becomes **706.63 & 76.05** buying 1/4 at capitulation, 1/4 on pullback, and final 1/2 at Dow theory buy signal.

	4/28/71	950.82	Market Highs		4/28	232.79		4/28	104.77		
	6/28/71	873.10	Pullback	-8.2%	6/28	208.89	-10.3%	6/22	97.59	-6.9%	
	7/12/71	903.40	Bounce	3.5%	7/12	220.21	5.4%	7/12	100.82	3.3%	

(continued)

Table 9.6 (continued)

Signal-Type (from Chapter 2)	Date:	DJ Ind.	%	Status:	Date:	DJ Trans	%	Date:	S&P500	%	Date:	% Better than Original Dow Theory Signals
Sell-1	**7/28/71**	**872.01**		Breakdown	7/28	208.06		7/28	97.07		7/28	**0.0%**
	7/28/71	**872.01**										
	8/10/71	839.59		Market Lows	8/4	203.61		8/9	93.53			
	9/8/71	920.53	9.7%	Bounce	9/7	248.33	22.0%	9/8	101.34	8.4%		
	11/23/71	797.97	-13.4%	New Low/Pullback	11/23	208.43	-16.1%	11/23	90.16	-11.0%		
Buy-2	**1/12/72**	**910.82**		Breakup	1/12	249.08		12/20	101.55			**1.1%**
	2/10/72	**921.28**						(1/12	(103.59)			
	1/11/73	1051.70		**Bull Market High**	12/11	240.41		1/11	120.24			
	2/27/73	947.72	-9.0%	Pullback	3/5	191.58	-20.3%	2/8	113.16	-5.9%		
	3/7/73	979.98	3.4%	Bounce	3/7	198.35	3.5%	2/13	116.78	3.2%		
Sell-1	**3/21/73**	**938.37**		Breakdown	3/23	189.22		2/26	112.19			**1.7%**
	3/23/73	**922.71**						(3/21	(110.49)			
	10/3/74	584.56		Market Lows	1/3	125.93		10/3	62.28			
	10/14/74	673.50	15.2%	Bounce	10/22	152.74	21.3%	10/21	73.50	18.0%		
	10/28/74	633.84	-5.9%	Pullback	10/28	145.78	-4.6%	10/28	70.09	-4.6%		
	11/5/74	674.75		Breakup	11/1	153.55		10/30	74.31			
Buy-1	**11/1/74**	**665.28***						(11/1	(73.88)			**3.0%**
	11/5/74	**674.75**										
	12/6/74	577.60		**Bear Market Low**								
	9/21/76	1014.79		**Bull Market High**	7/14	231.27		9/21	107.83			
	10/12/76	932.35	-8.1%	Pullback	10/12	203.85	-11.9%	11/10	98.81	-8.4%		
	12/31/76	1004.65	7.8%	Bounce/New High	5/18	246.64	21.00	12/31	107.46	8.8%		
	2/11/77	931.52		Breakdown	10/24	201.74		3/30	98.54			

*becomes **654.53 & 69.55** buying 1/4 at capitulation, 1/4 on pullback, and final 1/2 at Dow theory buy signal.

	Date	Value	%	Event	Date	Value	%	Date	Value	%	Signal %
Sell-2	**3/30/77**	**921.21**									**14.8%**
	10/24/77	**802.32**									(See Note 3)
	2/28/78	742.72		***Bear Market Low***	3/9	199.31		3/6	86.90		7.4%)
	5/17/78	858.37	15.6%	Bounce	5/22	231.30	16.1%	5/17	99.60	14.6%	
	5/26/78	831.69	-3.1%	Pullback	5/26	223.70	-3.3%	5/26	96.58	-3.0%	
Buy-1	**6/15/78**	**863.83**		Breakup	6/6	231.35		6/5	99.95		**0.3%**
	6/6/78	**866.51**									
	9/11/78	907.74		***Bull Market High***	9/8	261.49		9/12	106.99		
	9/20/78	857.16	-5.6%	Pullback	9/22	241.58	-7.6%	9/27	101.66	-5.0%	
	10/11/78	901.42	5.2%	Bounce	10/12	250.15	3.5%	10/11	105.39	3.7%	
	10/19/78	846.41		Breakdown	10/17	237.44		10/17	101.26		
Sell-1	**10/17/78**	**866.34**									**2.4%**
	10/19/78	**846.41**									
	11/14/78	785.26		Market Low/ ***Bear Market Low***	11/14	205.49		11/14	92.49		
	12/6/78	821.90	4.7%	Bounce	12/6	218.20	6.2%	12/6	97.49	5.4%	
	12/18/78	787.51	-4.2%	Pullback/New Low	12/20	203.45	-6.8%	12/18	93.44	-4.2%	
Buy-2	**1/4/79**	**826.14**		Breakup	1/15	218.79		12/26	97.52		**-1.1%**
	5/13/80	**816.89**						(1/4	98.58)		
	(4/21/80)	759.13		***Bear Low—DJIA only***	3/27	233.69		4/21	99.80)		
	4/27/81	1024.05		***Bull Market High***	4/16	447.38		11/28/80	140.52		
	5/11/81	963.44	-5.9%	Pullback	5/11	410.28	-8.3%	12/11	127.36	-9.4%	
	6/15/81	1011.99	5.0%	Bounce	6/1	430.92	5.0%	1/6	138.12	8.4%	
Sell-1	**7/2/81**	**959.19**		Breakdown	7/2	409.60		2/20	126.58		**0.0%**
	7/2/81	**959.19**						(7/2	128.64)		
	8/12/82	776.92		***Bear Market Low***	8/12	292.12		8/12	102.42		
	9/21/82	934.79	20.3%	Bounce	9/14	375.45	28.5%	9/21	124.88	21.9%	

(continued)

Table 9.6 *(continued)*

Signal-Type (from Chapter 2)	Date:	DJ Ind.	%	Status:	Date:	DJ Trans	%	Date:	S&P 500	%	% Better than Original Dow Theory Signals
Buy-1	9/30/82	896.25	-4.1%	Pullback	9/30	360.46	-4.0%	9/30	120.42	-3.6%	
	10/6/82	**944.26**		Breakup	10/7	382.87		10/6	125.97		**2.2%**
	10/7/82	**965.97**									
	11/29/83	1287.20		Market Highs	11/22	612.57		10/10	172.65		
	12/15/83	1236.79	-3.9%	Pullback	12/22	587.07	-4.2%	11/7	161.78	-6.3%	
	1/6/84	1286.64	4.0%	Bounce/**New High**	1/9	612.63	4.4%	11/29	167.91	3.8%	
Sell-2	**1/24/84**	**1242.88**		Breakdown	1/24	585.29		12/15	161.67		**0.9%**
	1/25/84	**1231.89**						(1/24	165.94)		
	7/24/84	1086.57		Market Lows	7/25	444.03		7/24	147.82		
	8/21/84	1239.73	14.1%	Bounce	9/14	526.52	18.6%	9/17	168.87	14.2%	
	10/9/84	1175.13	-5.2%	Pullback	10/9	508.48	-3.4%	10/9	161.87	-4.1%	
Buy-1	**11/6/84**	**1244.15**		Breakup	10/18	542.53		11/6	170.41		**1.4%**
	1/21/85	**1261.37**									
	8/25/87	2722.42		*Bull Market High*	8/14	1101.16		8/25	336.77		
	9/21/87	2492.82	-8.4%	Pullback	9/21	1005.80	-8.7%	9/21	310.54	-7.8%	
	10/2/87	2640.99	5.9%	Bounce	10/2	1064.41	5.8%	10/5	328.08	5.6%	
Sell-1	**10/14/87**	**2412.70**		Breakdown	10/15	980.24		10/12	309.39		**2.4%**
	10/15/87	**2355.09**						(10/14	305.23)		
	10/19/87	1738.74		*Bear Market Low*	10/20	740.25		10/19	224.84		
	10/21/87	2027.85	16.6%	Bounce	10/21	787.01	6.3%	10/21	258.38	15.4%	
	10/26/87	1793.93	-11.5%	Pullback/**New Low**	10/26	674.92	-14.2%	10/26	227.67	-11.9%	
	11/2/87	2014.09		Lower Bounce	11/2	784.38		11/2	255.75		
	12/4/87	1766.74		Pullback/**Lower Low**	12/4	661.00		12/4	223.92		

Signal	Date	Price	Pct	Description	Date	Price	Pct	Date	Price	Pct	Total
Buy-4	**1/5/88**	**2031.50***		Breakup	1/7	789.43		1/4	255.94		**8.7%**
	1/7/88	*2051.89*						(1/5	258.63)		

*becomes **1874.30 & 239.23** buying 1/4 at each capitulation, 1/4 on pullback, and final 1/4 at Dow theory buy.

Signal	Date	Price	Pct	Description	Date	Price	Pct	Date	Price	Pct	Total
	9/1/89	2752.09		Market Highs	9/5	1532.01		9/1	353.73		
	9/25/89	2659.19	−3.4%	Pullback	9/26	1424.96	−7.0%	9/14	343.16		
	1/9/89	2791.41	5.0%	**New High**/Bounce	10/9	1518.49	6.6%	10/9	359.80	4.8%	
Sell-2	**10/13/89**	**2569.26**		Breakdown	10/13	1406.29		10/13	333.62		**0.0%**
	10/13/89	*2569.29*									
	1/30/90	2543.24		Market Lows	1/30	1031.83		1/30	322.98		
	4/17/90	2765.77	8.7%	Bounce	3/27	1192.57	15.6%	4/16	344.74	6.7%	
	4/27/90	2645.05	−4.4%	Pullback	4/27	1128.20	−5.4%	4/27	329.11	−4.5%	
Buy-1	**5/11/90**	**2810.58**		Breakup	6/4	1207.85		5/11	352.00		**4.6%**
	6/4/90	*2935.19*									
	6/15/90	2935.89		Market Highs	6/6	1212.77		6/4	367.40		
	6/26/90	2842.33	−3.2%	Pullback	7/5	1131.02	−6.7%	6/26	352.06	−4.2%	
	7/16/90	2999.75	5.5%	**Bull Market High**/Bounce	7/16	1189.60	5.2%	1/16	368.95	4.8%	
Sell-2	**8/2/90**	**2864.60**		Breakdown	7/30	1125.00		8/2	351.48		**2.0%**
	8/3/90	*2809.65*									
	10/11/90	2365.10		*Bear Market Low*	10/17	821.93		10/11	295.46		
	10/19/90	2520.79	6.6%	Bounce	10/22	883.69	7.5%	10/22	314.76	6.5%	
	10/29/90	2430.20	−3.6%	Pullback	10/31	822.30	−6.9%	10/29	301.88	−4.1%	
Buy-1	**11/12/90**	**2540.35***		Breakup	12/5	903.67		11/12	319.48		**3.4%**
	12/5/90	*2610.40*									

*becomes **2520.61 & 314.38** buying 1/4 at capitulation, 1/4 on pullback, and final 1/2 at Dow theory buy signal.

Signal	Date	Price	Pct	Description	Date	Price	Pct	Date	Price	Pct	Total
	5/13/98	9211.84		Market Highs	4/16	3686.02		4/22	1130.54		
	6/15/98	8627.93	−6.3%	Pullback	6/2	3259.30	−11.6%	6/3	1082.73	−4.2%	
	7/17/98	9337.97	8.2%	**Bull Market High**/Bounce	7/14	3618.73	11.0%	7/17	1186.75	9.6%	

(continued)

Table 9.6 (continued)

Signal-Type (from Chapter 2)	Date:	DJ Ind.	%	Status;	Date:	DJ Trans	%	Date:	S&P 500	%	% Better than Original Dow Theory Signals
Sell-2	**8/4/98**	**8487.31**		Breakdown	7/29	3244.93		8/4	1072.12		**0.0%**
	8/4/06	**8487.31**									
	8/31/98	7539.07		**Bear Market Low**	9/4	2616.75		8/31	957.28		
	9/8/98	8020.78	6.4%	Bounce	9/8	2749.30	5.1%	9/8	1023.46	6.9%	
	9/10/98	7615.54	-5.4%	Pullback	9/10	2631.51	-4.3%	9/10	980.19	-4.2%	
Buy-1	**9/14/98**	**7945.35***		Breakup	9/14	2805.14		9/14	1029.72		**3.3%**
	9/15/98	**8024.39**									

*becomes **7761.33 & 999.23** buying 1/4 at capitulation, 1/4 on pullback, and final 1/2 at Dow theory buy signal.

Signal-Type (from Chapter 2)	Date:	DJ Ind.	%	Status;	Date:	DJ Trans	%	Date:	S&P 500	%	% Better than Original Dow Theory Signals
	5/13/99	11107.19		Market Highs	5/12	3783.50		5/13	1367.56		
	5/27/99	10466.93	-5.8%	Pullback	6/25	3316.11	-12.4%	6/1	1284.26	-6.1%	
	7/16/99	11209.84	7.1%	**New Highs**/Bounce	7/2	3515.99	6.0%	7/16	1418.78	10.5%	
	8/2/99	10645.96		Pullback/**Breakdown**	8/4	3280.07		8/10	1281.43		
	8/25/99	11326.04		**Market High**/Bounce	8/25	3309.25		8/25	1381.79		
Sell-3	**8/10/99**	**10655.15**		Breakdown							**3.3%**
	9/23/99	**10318.59**		**Bull Market High— Not DJTA** (See Note 4)	11/16/99	3099.67		3/24	1527.46)		
	(9/14/00)	11722.98									
	9/21/01	8235.81		**Bear Market Low**	9/20	2033.86		9/20	965.54		**3.8%**
	10/26/01	9545.17	15.9%	Bounce	10/11	2314.80	13.8%	10/26	1104.61	14.4%	
	10/31/01	9075.14	-4.9%	Pullback	10/19	2174.28	-6.1%	10/31	1059.78	-4.1%	
Buy-1	**11/6/01**	**9591.12***		Breakup	11/8	2320.98		11/6	1118.86		
	11/8/01	**9587.52**									

*becomes **9225.65 & 1078.48** buying 1/4 at capitulation, 1/4 on pullback, and final 1/2 at Dow theory buy signal.

Signal	Date	Dow	%	Event	Date	Nasdaq	%	Date	S&P	%	Return
	3/19/02	10635.25		**Bull Market High**	3/4	3049.96		3/19	1170.29		
	5/6/02	9808.04	−7.8%	Pullback	5/10	2643.10	−13.3%	5/7	1049.49	−10.3%	
	5/18/02	10353.08	5.6%	Bounce	5/17	2798.36	5.9%	5/17	1106.59	5.4%	
Sell-1	**6/3/02**	**9709.79**		Breakdown	6/25	2627.92		6/3	1040.68		
	6/25/02	*9126.80*									**6.4%**
	7/23/02	7702.34		Market Lows	7/23	2160.35		7/23	797.70		
	7/31/02	8736.59	13.4%	Bounce	7/30	2389.51	10.6%	7/31	911.62	14.3%	
	8/5/02	8043.63	−7.9%	Pullback/**New Low**	8/5	2132.27	−10.8%	8/5	834.60	−8.4%	
	8/9/02	8745.45		Breakup	8/21	2423.21		8/14	919.62		
Buy-2	**8/14/02**	**8743.31***									
	8/21/02	*8957.23*									**5.1%**

*becomes **8503.13 & 892.91** buying 1/4 at capitulation, 1/4 on pullback, and final 1/2 at Dow theory buy signal.

Signal	Date	Dow	%	Event	Date	Nasdaq	%	Date	S&P	%	Return
	8/22/02	9053.64		Market Highs	8/22	2463.96		8/22	962.70		
	9/5/02	8283.70	−8.5%	Pullback	9/5	2204.26	−10.5%	9/3	878.02	−8.8%	
	9/10/02	8602.61	3.8%	Bounce	9/11	2297.32	4.2%	9/10	909.58	3.6%	
Sell-1	**9/17/02**	**8207.55**		Breakdown	9/16	2203.69		9/17	873.52		
	9/17/02	*8207.55*									**0.0%**
	10/9/02	7286.27		**Bear Market Low**	1/9	2013.02		10/9	776.76		
	10/21/02	8538.24	17.2%	Bounce	10/23	2341.55	16.3%	10/21	899.72	15.8%	
	10/24/02	8317.34	−2.6%	Pullback	10/29	2248.23	−4.0%	10/24	882.50	−1.9%	
Buy-1	**11/4/02**	**8571.60***		Breakup	11/5	2344.46		11/1	900.96		
	11/5/02	*8678.27*						(11/4)	(908.35)		**7.1%**

*becomes **8061.52 & 868.90** from retained 1/4 from 1st capitulation, add 1/4 at 2nd capitulation, 1/4 on pullback, and final 1/4 at Dow theory buy signal.

Signal	Date	Dow	%	Event	Date	Nasdaq	%	Date	S&P	%	Return
	11/27/02	8931.68		Market Highs	11/6	2413.71		11/27	938.87		
	12/27/02	8303.78	−7.0%	Pullback	1/11	2268.35	−6.0%	12/27	875.40	−6.8%	
	1/14/03	8842.62	6.5%	Bounce/**New High**	1/6	2421.71	6.8%	1/14	931.66	6.4%	

(continued)

Table 9.6 (continued)

Signal-Type (from Chapter 2)	Date:	DJ Ind.	%	Status:	Date:	DJ Trans	%	Date:	S&P 500	%	% Better than Original Dow Theory Signals
Sell-2	**1/24/03**	**8131.01**		Breakdown	1/22	2213.63		1/24	861.40		**0.0%**
	1/24/03	*8131.01*									
	3/11/03	7524.06		*Market Low/**Bear Market Low***	3/11	1942.19		3/11	800.73		
	3/21/03	8521.97	13.3%	Bounce	3/21	2263.49	16.5%	3/21	895.79	11.9%	
	3/31/03	7992.13	-6.2%	Pullback	3/31	2131.21	-5.8%	3/31	848.14	-5.3%	
Buy-1	**4/22/03**	**8484.99**		Breakup	4/15	2316.62		4/22	911.37		**1.1%**
	5/2/03	*8582.68*									
	2/11/04	10737.70		Market Highs	1/22	3080.32		2/11	1157.76		
	3/24/04	10048.23	-6.4%	Pullback	3/22	2750.80	-10.7%	3/24	1091.19	-5.7%	
	4/6/04	10570.81	5.2%	Bounce	4/22	3006.76	9.3%	4/5	1150.57	5.4%	
Sell-1	**5/10/04**	**9990.02**		Breakdown	none	none		5/10	1087.12		(See Note 5)
	none	*none*									
	8/12/04	9814.59		Market Lows	8/6	2966.08		8/12	1063.23		
	9/14/04	10318.16	5.1%	Bounce	10/6	3388.72	14.3%	10/6	1142.05	7.4%	
	10/25/04	9749.49	-5.5%	**New Low**/Pullback	10/13	3282.43	-3.1%	1/25	1094.80	-4.1%	
Buy-2	**11/3/04**	**10137.05**		Breakup	10/21	3431.69		11/3	1143.20		**-1.5%***
	7/19/07	14000.14		Market Highs	7/19	5446.49		7/19	1553.08		
	8/3/07	13181.9	-5.60%	Pullback	8/3	4873.81	-10.50%	8/3	1433.06	-7.7	
	8/8/2007	13657.86	3.60%	Bounce	8/8	5079.39	4.20%	8/8	1497.49	4.50%	

Sell-1	**8/14/07**	**13028.92**	Breakdown	8/14	4850.25	8/14	1426.54	**1.80%**
	11/21/07	**12799.04**						
	10/9/07	14164.53	**Bull Market Highs— Not DJTA** (See Note 6)	10/5	4997.17	10/9	1565.15	

Average Signal Improvement:	**2.20%**

* −1.5% is the loss between the previous sell and this buy in the absence of any original Dow Theory signals.

Note 1. At the time of the signal, the DJTA was "seriously" diverging by 8.1% so I only acted on half the new signal and waited on the final half for the DJTA to confirm; consequently the sell was adjusted to midway between the new and the old signal levels for a 454.72 average cost and only a 1.1% better price level. When the Transports have to move as much as 8 to 10%, I would wait on half for confirmation.

Note 2. Same as Note 1; the DJTA was diverging by 11.1% so I held off on the final. in this case, quarter, purchase, for a 713.42 average cost and only a 6.0% better price level.

Note 3. Similar to Notes 1 and 2; the DJTA was diverging by 9.7% so I delayed the final half sale made for an 861.77 average sale level and only a 7.4% better price.

Note 4. After the sell signal, both the DJIA and S&P 500 rose to new highs, extending the bull market. However, the DJTA did not participate. After a long bull market, you do not want to be aggressive in chasing it without confirmation by all three indices. Therefore, on type B-5 buy signals (at new highs), wait for full confirmation of all three indices before buying.

Note 5. Although the divergence of the DJTA was only 2.1%, nonetheless it never confirmed the DJIA and S&P 500. I did not act on this signal and advised my subscribers to stay in the buy mode that the Dow Theory and my other indicators were still signaling. Two of the capitulation indicators had recently given buy signals, and I wrote that I was expecting a multiyear bull market for numerous reasons. Had the DJTA broken down, I would have honored that signal.

Note 6. Same as Note 4.

individual improvement is relatively small, but it is the accumulation of those improvements that adds up to a real increase in the results. The average annual gain from buy to sell for this Dow Theory for the twenty-first century is an almost 3 percent better annual gain than the original Dow Theory's results.

The notes to the table are an important part of the record. You'll notice that I dwell on the action of the DJTA (Dow Jones Transportation Average) even though its confirmation of a new Dow Theory signal is not always necessary. When it is "seriously diverging," I give it the benefit of the doubt and only act on half the signal given without its participation or, in the case of B-5 buy signals, wait for all three indices to come into agreement.

Also, recall from Chapter 2 that in the absence of any other type of Dow Theory buy signal, the attainment of "new all-time highs" would constitute a buy signal. In my interpretation of the Dow Theory for the twenty-first century, I have added that all three indices must confirm such a signal. Examples of the wisdom of this tweaking of the rules are evident in avoiding the false breakouts to new highs after Dow Theory sell signals in both 1999 and 2007.

Bold dates and Dow Jones levels in the table are new signals; bold italicized just below them are the Dow Theory dates and Dow Jones levels not utilizing the S&P 500.

In addition to the Dow Theory, new or old, there are other important indicators that you should be aware of in order to understand, anticipate, and profit in the stock market. We cover those indicators in the chapters to come.

PART

IV

OTHER IMPORTANT INDICATORS

CHAPTER

10

Schannep Timing Indicator

THE OTHER MAJOR-TREND INDICATOR

In this chapter, we discuss the Tucson Indicator and how it developed into the major trend indicator at a major brokerage firm. During my business career at Dean Witter (now Morgan Stanley), the Computer Assistance to Research (COMPARE) department developed a number of computer-generated programs as an aid to analysts and brokers in identifying attractive industry groups for investment. I saw certain patterns in their output that coincided with bull and bear markets occurring. Because I was in charge of the Tucson and southern Arizona offices, it was originally referred to as the Tucson indicator. After the firm shut down that part of the technical analysis operation, I continued to experiment and streamlined it into the Schannep Timing Indicator. You should know about it because, like the Dow Theory, it has an excellent record.

Combining the Factors to Create a Bull or Bear Market

Over the years, I have observed that while no two bull or bear markets are ever exactly alike, *certain ingredients must be present for them to form.* As a young flight instructor in the air force, I taught meteorology for a time. In thunderstorms, it was obvious that a combination of factors had to come together for them to form. It wasn't just moisture in the air or moisture aloft at higher altitudes that was required, but also a source of lift. Air needed to be lifted, by passing over a mountain range, by summer heating of the ground below, or by a cold frontal system moving in under the existing warmer air. That combination, with a little help from unstable air and Zeus, the ruler of the celestial realm, usually caused cumulus clouds, which then developed into thunderstorms. And then the thunder and lightning began!

Likewise, a combination of factors must come together at the same time to form either a bull or bear market. First, a *momentum* must begin upward in the case of a bull market or downward in the case of a bear. The critical factor is whether that movement is just a jiggle or is of adequate strength to build into a genuine bull or bear market. Variation away from an existing trend can be measured by the same short-term oscillator described in the formal paper shown in Chapter 7. When the positive or negative momentum trend reaches a 1 percent threshold of change, it can be judged to be likely to continue. An analogy would be an aircraft careening down the runway. Until it reaches a certain threshold it is just speeding; after that, it is flying.

In addition to momentum, the second ingredient is a *monetary atmosphere* conducive to fueling a bull market or contributing to a bear market. Fortunately, the atmosphere can be determined to be favorable, neutral, or unfavorable, adding to or detracting from the likelihood of the momentum developing further into a bull or bear market. To determine the status of the monetary situation, I look to the Fed Funds rate and the free reserves levels to determine the cost of money as to being cheap or dear and its availability. Both are used to ascertain a favorable, neutral, or unfavorable monetary status. The Federal Reserve Open Market Committee sets the target interest rate that banks pay for overnight borrowing. Those rates, known as the Fed Funds rates, can be found in the *Wall Street Journal.* If banks have more reserves than required by the Federal Reserve, those are called free reserves.

Another Indicator for Predicting the Stock Market

Everyone realizes that although the future is not knowable, some things are predictable. The purpose of my Stock Market Major Trend Timing Indicator is to identify changes in the trend of price movements on the major stock averages. It has been said many times in Dean Witter publications that *"the genius of investing is recognizing the direction of a trend—not catching the highs or lows.*" Although history gives some parameters, neither the duration nor the extent of the move can be predicted in advance. *None* of the input that goes into my indicator is from forecasts; *all* is from existing printed public information. I would like to give Dean Witter credit for believing in investment timing as evidenced in the company's 1975 booklet, "Will COMPARE Improve Your Sense of Timing?" The booklet states, "Dean Witter believes timing— knowing *when to buy and when to sell*—is one of the most important factors in any investment decision."

Dean Witter was not the first to believe in timing. Over 60 years ago, in 1945, an advertisement by Merrill Lynch, Pierce, Fenner & Beane stated:

> With world-shaking events a commonplace many an investor seeks an investment guidepost, realizes now more than ever that *when to buy ranks equally in importance with what to buy*. Too, wise investors also know that no security today can be bought and forgotten, that successful investment practice requires keen judgment in timing sales as well as purchases.

As data became available on a more timely basis from the Federal Reserve Board, I have been able to generate the necessary calculations on my own computer. I have streamlined, refined, and made my indicator more time responsive than its rudimentary start in 1969. While the makeup of the momentum component of my indicator is mathematically challenging, the monetary part is quite simple. Nonetheless, it is not subject to individual interpretation, as the Dow Theory is. My CPA is privy to my indicator's very specific construction and had no trouble certifying its signal dates without contradiction with my own interpretation. That certification can be found in Appendix D.

While the signal dates in my Schannep Timing Indicator and the Dow Theory are similar, they are constructed in totally different ways. My indicator is constructed through mathematical calculations of *internal* momentum and monetary atmosphere, whereas the Dow Theory is totally determined by the external chart patterns. In my humble opinion, these are the two premier stock market major trend timing indicators with documented and verified long-term records which set the standard for market timing.

So how does it work out in the stock market? Table 10.1 shows the results for the Standard & Poor's 500 Index three months, six months, nine months, and a year after buy signals with the average gains being +7.8 percent, +14.9 percent, +18.0 percent, and +22.2 percent, excluding dividends. The average annual gain from buy to sell was 17.0 percent including dividends.

In Table 10.1, I have incorporated capitulation as a partial buy indicator. As with the Dow Theory, a Schannep Timing Indicator buy signal has always followed capitulation. Therefore, when it does occur, I enter into a half purchase position, and if it repeats (as it has done three times now in the last 50 years), I bring the position up to two-thirds invested. The different percentages from those used with the Dow Theory are because there is no requirement that a pullback follow, as with the Dow Theory. Therefore, the only other opportunity to add to the position would be when the Schannep Timing Indicator signal is completed at the signal date shown in the table. At that time, the final purchase to bring the position to 100 percent invested is made.

Author's note: A buy on 4/6/01 (not shown) was a result of reinstating an erroneous sell caused by the Federal Reserve correcting its reported figures and is therefore not included with the other bona-fide buy signals.

The results following sell signals are shown in Table 10.2.

Author's notes: When no "official" bear market follows, the market level marked with an asterisk is the low for this move. The sell on 8/5/2004 marked with a double asterisk was treated as a half sell signal at the time due to the very favorable monetary atmosphere then existing, so it is weighted at half the others. Eleven signals were followed by official bear markets, eight were not. (The eight are indicated by the asterisk in Table 10.2.)

The results for this indicator are very similar to those for the Dow Theory results, quite coincidentally. As this indicator is determined almost solely by calculations of momentum with concern for the monetary situation, quite unlike the chart pattern analysis required by the Dow Theory, it might be surprising that the results are so similar. The advantage of using these two premier indicators together is that you arrive at similar conclusions in totally different ways. The complete record with dates and market levels of buy and sell signals over the last 50+ years is shown in Appendix D, where it is a part of the Composite Indicator. There you will see

Table 10.1 Schannep Timing Indicator Buy Signals and the S&P 500 Gain Thereafter (data since December 31, 1953)

Date	Level	3 Months: Level	Gain	6 Months: Level	Gain	9 Months: Level	Gain	1 year: Level	Gain	To Sell Signal: Sell Date	Level	Gain
1/25/1954	25.93	27.76	7.1%	30.31	16.9%	31.96	23.3%	35.51	36.9%	8/20/1956	48.25	86.1%
5/5/1958	43.79	47.75	9.0%	52.03	18.8%	54.81	25.2%	57.75	31.9%	11/12/1959	57.17	30.6%
1/3/1961	57.57	65.6	13.9%	65.21	13.3%	67.77	17.7%	71.13	23.6%	5/10/1962	63.57	10.4%
11/14/1962	56.42	66.35	17.6%	70.21	24.4%	71.07	26.0%	72.95	29.3%	5/2/1966	90.9	61.1%
12/27/1966	81.00	90.87	12.2%	91.30	12.7%	96.79	19.5%	95.91	18.4%	1/22/1968	94.03	16.1%
4/11/1968	96.53	102.39	6.1%	108.18	12.1%	100.93	4.6%	98.65	2.2%	3/7/1969	98.65	2.2%
8/24/1970	75.62	84.78	12.1%	96.73	27.9%	100.13	32.4%	100.40	32.8%	2/23/1973	113.16	49.6%
10/22/1973	109.16									11/20/1973	98.66	-9.6%
11/4/1974	70.73	77.61	9.7%	89.22	26.1%	87.15	23.2%	88.51	25.1%	10/31/1977	92.34	30.6%
4/17/1978	94.45	97.78	3.5%	101.26	7.2%	96.03	1.7%			10/26/1978	96.03	1.7%
6/11/1980	116.02	125.66	8.3%	127.36	9.8%	129.95	12.0%	133.80	15.3%	8/31/1981	122.79	5.8%
8/23/1982	116.11	132.93	14.5%	146.79	26.4%	163.43	40.8%	162.80	40.2%	2/22/1984	154.31	32.9%
8/21/1984	167.83	164.52	-2.0%	180.19	7.4%	189.64	13.0%	189.20	12.7%	10/16/1987	282.7	68.4%
3/16/1988	239.57	269.77	12.6%	270.65	13.0%	276.29	15.3%	299.40	25.0%	8/24/1990	311.51	30.0%
1/25/1991	321.57	379.25	17.9%	380.96	18.5%	384.2	19.5%	415.00	29.1%	6/20/1994	455.48	41.6%
2/22/1995	485.07	523.65	8.0%	559.52	15.3%	598.4	23.4%	658.90	35.8%	8/27/1998	1042.6	114.9%
11/5/1998	1045.6	1239.4	18.5%	1347.30	28.9%	1313.71	25.6%	1324.00	26.6%	8/30/1999	1324.02	26.6%
12/3/1999	1433.3	1409.2	-1.7%	1477.30	3.1%	1520.77	6.1%	1315.00	-8.2%	7/3/2002	953.99	-33.4%
11/5/2002	858.47	843.59	-1.7%	926.55	7.9%	965.46	12.5%	1052.00	22.5%	8/5/2004	1080.7	25.9%
11/22/2004*	1170.30	1201.60	2.7%	1189.30	1.6%	1219.71	4.2%	1255.00	7.2%	7/12/2006	1258.6	7.5%
10/12/2006	1362.83	1430.73	5.0%	1447.80	6.2%	1547.8	13.6%	1561.80	14.6%	1/15/2008	1380.95	1.3%
Average:			7.8%		14.9%		18.0%		22.2%			28.6%

Table 10.2   Schannep Timing Indicator Sell Signals and the Further S&P 500 Loss to the Final Bear Market Lows (data since December 31, 1953)

Sell Date	Level	Low Date	Level	Further Loss	Months to Low
8/20/1956	48.25	10/22/1957	38.98	19.2%	14.1
11/12/1959	57.17	10/25/1960	52.30*	8.5%	11.5
5/10/1962	63.57	6/26/1962	52.32	17.7%	1.5
5/2/1966	90.90	10/7/1966	73.20	19.5%	5.2
1/22/1968	94.03	3/5/1968	87.72*	6.7%	1.5
3/7/1969	98.65	5/26/1970	69.29	29.8%	14.6
2/23/1973	113.16	8/22/1973	100.53*	11.2%	6.0
11/20/1973	98.66	10/3/1974	62.28	36.9%	10.5
10/31/1977	92.34	3/6/1978	86.90	5.9%	4.2
10/26/1978	96.03	11/14/1978	92.49*	3.7%	0.6
8/31/1981	122.79	8/12/1982	102.42	16.6%	11.4
2/22/1984	154.31	7/24/1984	147.82*	4.2%	5.1
10/16/1987	282.70	12/4/1987	223.92	20.8%	1.6
8/24/1990	311.51	10/11/1990	295.46	5.2%	1.6
6/20/1994	455.48	6/24/1994	442.80*	2.8%	0.1
8/27/1998	1042.59	8/31/1998	957.28	8.2%	0.1
8/30/1999	1324.02	10/15/1999	1247.41*	5.8%	1.5
8/5/2004**	1080.70	8/12/2004	1063.23*	1.6%	0.3
7/12/2006	1258.60	7/17/06	1234.49*	1.9%	0.2
1/15/2008	1380.95				
	Average further decline:			**12.5%**	**4.9**

how the Schannep Timing Indicator and the Dow Theory work in tandem. I have not included a graphic as was done for the Dow Theory because the results are so close. In Chapter 13 we will see just how well capitulation, the Dow Theory, this indicator, and the definitions of bull and bear work in conjunction with one another. But first we look at some other important indicators in the next two chapters.

CHAPTER

11

"Three Tops and a Tumble"

LEADING TOPPING INDICATORS

*F*oretelling stock market tops is the hardest part of market timing. That being said, in this chapter we discuss three indicators that have an excellent record of identifying market tops. *Three recurring phenomena* are helpful in forecasting market tops: New York Stock Exchange (NYSE) volume peaks, an inverted yield curve, and consumer confidence tops. When these three indicators top out, the market is usually not far behind. Then introduce another top—housing—that often has an impact on forecasting markets. Let's take a look at them. I'm sure you'll see what I mean.

Recurring Phenomenon #1: Volume Peaks

The largest monthly volume *during* a bull market (after it is "official." based on my definition in Chapter 1) tends to occur on average five months *ahead* of the market's top. Each month has its own number of trading days due to holidays, how weekends fall, and so on (with February always having less than any other.) Therefore, it is most appropriate to use the month with the *highest average volume per day*.

In December 1999, NYSE monthly volume was a recorded for the then-existing bull market (see Table 11.1). Therefore, an investor should have started looking for a stock market top over the following five months. The Dow Jones topped that next month. *After* the bull market top, any higher volume, such as occurred in

Table 11.1   Relationship of Volume and Market Tops

Bear Market Low (Mo/Yr)	"Official" Bull Market	High Volume (Mo/Yr)	Stock Market Top (Mo/Yr)	Lead Time
9/1900	12/00 est.	4/01	6/01	2 mos.
11/03	7/04*	1/06	1/06	0
11/07	1/08*	11/08	11/09	12
9/11	3/12*	4/12	9/12	5
12/14	4/15*	11/16	11/16	0
12/17	1/18*	10/19	11/19	1
8/21	11/21*	4/22	3/23	11
10/23	7/24*	10/29	9/29	1 (lag)
7/32	7/32 Actual	3/33*	3/37	48*
3/38	4/38	10/38	11/38	1
4/42	10/42	1/46	5/46	4
6/49	11/49	12/54	4/56	16
10/57	7/58	3/61	12/61	9
6/62	11/62	12/65	2/66	2
10/66	4/67	4/68	12/68	8
5/70	9/70	11/72	1/73	2
12/74	1/75	1/76	9/76	8
2/78	8/78	8/78	9/78	1
4/80	7/80	3/81	3/81	1
8/82	9/82	8/87	8/87	0
10/87	2/88	6/88	7/90	25
10/90	2/91	7/98	7/98	0
8/98	11/98	12/99	1/00	1
9/01	11/01	1/02	3/02	2
10/02	11/02	8/07	10/07	2 mos.
			Average:	**5 mos.**

*This was the high-volume month *during* the erratic markets associated with the depression and its aftermath (when numerous mini–bull and mini–bear markets occurred in the 1929 to 1937 period shown in Chapter 7) and are considered to have been aberrations. Their average lead time of volume highs to market tops during those times was less than one month. This is not included in the average lead time calculation.

January and March of 2001, is of no help in determining that bear market's duration. The same thing happened in January of 2008 after the October 2007 top. If the market had not gone into a bear market, then that month's volume would come into play in a continuing bull market.

Bottom Line

Volume almost always peaks at or before the stock market does. *Even higher volume can, of course, follow* the "record" volume as a bull market continues on. *During* bull markets investors watch for volume to top, as it did in January of 2002 before the March 2002 top. Record volume months can be found on the NYSE Web site.

Recurring Phenomenon #2: Inverted Yield Curve

As I mentioned at the beginning of this chapter, foretelling stock market tops is the hardest part of market timing. There is, however, something about the yield curve that can be very helpful in that regard. Long-term interest rates are usually higher than short-term rates. The simple explanation is that long-term lenders demand a premium to compensate for expected probable inflation, whereas short-term rates don't usually face that prospect. Sometimes that relationship is reversed due to a combination of factors not easily explained: perhaps the Federal Reserve Board has increased short-term rates to slow an overexuberant economy and long-term holders expect the Fed to be successful and therefore do not demand any premium. There are other possible reasons, but the fact is sometimes short rates rise to a level higher than long rates, and when it does, it is described as an inverted yield curve.

The actual definition of the yield curve uses various interest rates, from the 3-month Treasury bill versus the 10-year note, or the 20-year bonds, even the 30-year bonds. Some use the 1-year note versus the 10-year note, others the 2-year or the 5-year or 10-year versus the 30-year note. My research shows that the relationship between the 3-month bill and 10-year notes is the most useful, as does the New York Federal Reserve Bank. The 10-year Treasuries have become the benchmark of the bond market. Whichever definition you choose, the results of a flattening to inverted yield curve are the same: a slowing economy at best and a depression at worst, but usually a recession.

I recommend a 1996 study by the New York Federal Reserve Bank covering the previous 35 years as an excellent background piece. (See http://www.newyorkfed.org/research/current_issues/ci2-7.pdf.) Its "Estimated Recession Probabilities for Profit Model Using the Yield Curve Spread" four quarters ahead, using the spread between the interest rates on the 10-year Treasury note and the 3-month Treasury bill, are shown in Table 11.2.

Table 11.2   Recession Probabilities

Recession Probability (%)	Value of Spread (Percentage Points)
10	0.76
15	0.46
20	0.22
25	0.02
30	−0.17
40	−0.50
50	−0.82
60	−1.13
70	−1.46
80	−1.85
90	−2.40

Toward the end of the year 2000, the spread approached a negative −0.90 points, implying over a 50 percent chance of recession, up from a just a 10 percent chance at the start of 2000. A recession began in March of 2001 and ended in November of 2001.

A February 2006 Federal Reserve working paper, "The Yield Curve and Predicting Recessions," has updated the earlier study and concluded that chances of recession are lower if Fed Funds rates are low and higher if they are high. The Federal Reserve Open Market Committee sets the target interest rate for the Fed Funds rates, and they are usually similar to the three-month Treasury note yield. The point of the update is to prove that the economy works better in a low-interest-rate environment and recessions are more likely when interest rates are high.

In March 2006, the 3-month Treasury note average rate was 4.51 percent and the 10-year Treasury bond rate was 4.72 percent. Using the 0.21 spread between the two at some other date when Fed Funds were at a 3.5 percent level would put the chances of recession at 17 percent as opposed to the 20 percent shown in Table 11.2. Alternately, if Fed Funds are 5.5 percent and the spread is the same 0.21 percent, then the chances double to 35 percent. This new information seems to endorse the approach I have used for many years.

My work encompasses the past 47 years, from 1953 to the present, and uses the *monthly* average 3-month Treasury bill rate *divided by* the

10-year Treasury bond yield. It is evident that as the *ratio,* as opposed to the *spread* used by the Federal Reserve, reaches or exceeds **0.95 percent,** the economy drops into an official recession or at least a serious slowdown approximately a year later. In 2001, the ratio not only exceeded 0.95 percent, but the 3-month yield exceeded the 10-year yield by a considerable amount. The recession lasted from March through November 2001. In early and mid-2006, the ratio once again exceeded 0.95 percent, and in late 2006 and early 2007, the 3-month yield exceeded the 10-year yield, just as it did in 2001. As an example of how lower interest rates might impact the recession probability, consider the following: Dividing a 3-month yield of 4.70 percent by a 5.00 percent yield for the 10-year yield equals **0.94 percent,** right at the 0.95 percent danger number. Now use the same 0.30 spread at 3 percent lower levels, such as 1.70 percent for the 3-month yield and 2.00 percent for the 10-year yield. Dividing 1.70 by 2.00 equals **0.85 percent,** which would not have been at the danger number. (See Figure 11.1.)

Think there'll never be another recession? History doesn't support that conclusion. Table 11.3 shows the results of flattening.

Bottom Line

A flattening or inverted yield curve points to a bear market and a coming recession. It usually leads by some six months on average,

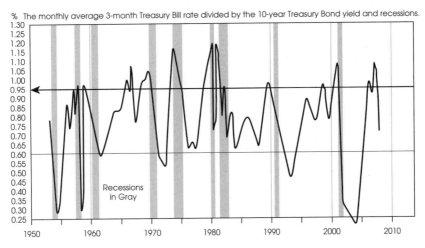

Figure 11.1 Yield Curve and Recessions

Table 11.3 Inverted Yield Curves over the Last 100-plus Years

Month/Year		Months	Stock Market		Bear	Months	Recessions	
Start	End	Lead to>	High	Low	Decline	Lead to>	Start	End
6/1900	3/03	12	6/01	11/03	46%	27	9/02	8/04
7/04	6/08	18	1/06	11/07	49	34	5/07	6/08
1/10	6/10	22	11/09	9/11	27	0	1/10	1/12
7/12	6/13	−2	9/12	7/14	25	6	1/13	12/14
6/18	12/20	17	11/19	8/21	47	2	8/18	3/19
5/27	4/29	28	9/29	7/32	89	27	8/29	3/33
2/57**	3/57	−10	4/56	10/57	19	6	8/57	4/58
12/59	1/60	1	1/60	10/60	17*	4	4/60	2/61
1/66	3/67	1	2/66	10/66	25	11	12/66***	6/67
4/68	4/70	8	12/68	5/70	36	20	12/69	11/70
6/73	1/75	−5	1/73	12/74	45	5	11/73	3/75
11/78	5/80	−2	9/78	4/80	16	14	1/80	7/80
10/80**	10/81	6	4/81	8/82	24	9	7/81	11/82
4/89	1/90	15	7/90	10/90	21	15	7/90	3/91
9/98	1/99	−2	7/98	8/98	19	30	3/01	11/01
and7/00	3/01	−6	1/00	9/01	30	8	3/01	11/01
1/06	7/07	3	10/07					

Average lead: 6.5 mos. to Bear Market.   **Average lead: 13.6 mos. to recession**

*Correction only (S&P 500 did not drop 16 percent).
**Also 12/57 and 2/82.
***"Growth" recession (not an official recession) when industrial production dropped for two quarters.

but in one-third of the previous occurrences, a bear market had already started, although none was yet defined or recognized by the date of the flattening or inversion shown. The lead time prior to the onset of a recession has been just over a year on average, and in **15 out of 16 (94 percent) flattenings/inversions, an official recession has followed**. An inverted yield curve is a far better predictor than are bear markets, which *usually* are followed by recession (17 of 22, or 77 percent in the twentieth century). I agree with the Federal Reserve Bank of New York when it said: "Forecasting with the yield curve has the distinct advantage of being quick and simple."

Recurring Phenomenon #3: Consumer Confidence

Consumer confidence is important because two-thirds of the American economy is impacted by the consumer. The Conference Board's monthly index measuring the economic outlook of 5,000 households is considered a predictor of future spending and hence economic growth. Its actual record in that regard is suspect, at best. What is of more interest to investors is its relationship to the stock market. Since the index was created in 1967, it has fluctuated between 43 and 145.

Until the year 2000, the *previous all-time high* of the index was in October of 1968 at 142.3. The bull market as measured by the Dow Jones *topped out five weeks later* on December 3, at 985, before dropping 36 percent over the next 18 months to 631. A recession started a year later in December 1969. The *all-time low* on the index was in December 1974 at 43.2, and the bear market *bottomed that month* on December 6, at 577, before rising 75 percent over the next 21 months. A five-year economic expansion began three months later in March 1975.

It would appear that the stock market has an important bearing on consumers' confidence levels; confidence is highest near market highs and lowest near market lows. Can you believe that the Conference Board's director of consumer research has said that "stocks don't play a big role in consumer confidence" (Dow Jones Newswires, 12/28/99)? Much has been written about the effects of fear and greed on the stock market, and indeed, investors'/consumers' confidence is similarly affected. So just how good is the relationship between high confidence (greed?) and bull market tops, and low confidence (fear?) and bear market bottoms? Let's look at the peaks and valleys (which I define as *separated by at least 32 ½ points*) of consumer confidence over the last 39 years, and their relationship to the stock market's highs and lows and the economy's ups and downs (see Figure 11.2).

In Table 11.4, you can see the dates and levels when consumer confidence reached prior peaks. It shows the lead time to the then existing bull market's approaching top as well as the lead time to the next recession.

There were *no other such peaks* meeting the definition in the time frame shown, including none ahead of the 9/76 to 2/78, 8/87 to 10/87, or 7/98 to 8/98 bear markets. Interestingly, those three bear markets were the *only* ones since the index was started that were not followed by recessions. When the index has peaked, *in all cases* to date, a bear market and recession have followed. Bear markets *usually* "forecast" recessions; index peaking *always* has!

Unfortunately, the valleys in consumer confidence do not lead the beginning of bull markets, as you can see in Table 11.5.

The saying goes "It is always darkest just before the dawn." Actually, investors stay in a funk until *after* bear markets end and a new bull market is already under way. All of the valleys shown in Table 11.5 involved recessions, with three occurring during recessions and two after the recessions had ended. There were no other valleys followed by the increase in consumer confidence that would qualify them as confidence valleys.

The monthly report comes out on the last Tuesday of the month *during the month that is covered*, with any revision made the following

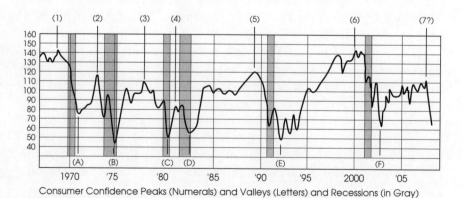

Consumer Confidence Peaks (Numerals) and Valleys (Letters) and Recessions (in Gray)

Figure 11.2   Consumer Confidence and Recessions

Table 11.4   Relationship of Confidence Peaks to Bull Market Peaks and Recessions

Consumer Confidence Peaks (Mo/Yr)	Lead Time (in months) to	Bull Market Highs (Date and Level)	Confidence Peak Lead Time (in months) to	Recession's Start (Mo/Yr)
1. 10/68 @ 142.3	2	12/68 @ 985	14	12/69
2. 12/72 @ 116.1	1	1/73 @ 1052	11	11/73
3. 4/78 @ 109.9	5	9/78 @ 908	21	1/80
4. 11/80 @ 87.2	5	4/81 @ 1024	8	7/81
5. 2/89 @120.7	17	7/90 @ 3000	17	7/90
6. 1&5/00 @144.7	0	1/00 @ 11723	10	3/01
7. 7/07 @ 112.6		10/07 @ 14164	5?	12/07?
Average:	**4.5 months**	**Average:**	**12.0 months**	

Table 11.5   Relationship of Confidence Valleys to Bear Market Lows and Recessions Endings

Consumer Confidence Valleys (Mo/Yr)	(Lag) to Months	Bear Market Lows (Date and Level)	Confidence Valley Lead (Lag) to (months)	Start of Economic Expansion
A. 4/71 @ 75.2	(11)	5/70 @ 631	(5)	11/70
B. 12/74 @ 43.2	0	12/74 @ 578	3	3/75
C. 5/80 @ 50.1	(1)	4/80 @ 759	2	7/80
D. 10/82 @ 54.3	(2)	8/82 @ 777	1	11/82
E. 2/92 @ 47.3	(16)	10/90 @ 2365	(11)	3/91
F. 3/03 @ 61.4	(5)	10/02 @ 7286	(16)	11/01
Average:	**6-month lag**	**Average:**	**4-month lag**	

month. While a peak or valley is not always definitive until later, *the fact that it is not surpassed in subsequent months is a clue of its reversal.*

The University of Michigan's Consumer Sentiment is a very similar index whose results closely approximate, but are not the same as, those of the Conference Board. This index started earlier in 1952. Its valleys preceded the economic expansion starting May 1954 by six months and the expansion beginning April 1958 by two months. It did not "forecast" the one starting in February 1961. Its peak preceded the recession starting August 1957 by nine months but missed the one starting April 1960. The advantage of the Consumer

Sentiment index, however, is that it is released approximately two weeks earlier each month than the Conference Board's release and is often a clue as to what to expect from an upcoming consumer confidence report. A "Small Business Optimism Index" is also released monthly and can be a guide to confidence. Consumer confidence as measured by the Conference Board since 1967 has been an *excellent forecasting tool and the one that I follow most closely.*

Bottom Line

Consumer confidence typically rises during bull markets, which is probably a reflection of what is often called the wealth effect. That confidence usually reaches a peak some five months on average before the stock market peaks. A recession follows eight months on average after that. The index peaks at an average level of 120.2, with 87.2 being the lowest peak. Conversely, consumers become less confident and concern turns to fear even after the bear market has ended and a new bull market has begun, which in turn signals the start of an economic expansion. The index valleys at an average level of 54, with 75.2 being the highest valley.

The Consumer Confidence Index is published monthly for the entire world to see, but it's important to know that it is a far better gauge of when the stock market and the economy will *change* rather than what they will *continue* to do. Its tops lead at stock market tops, much as volume tops and an inverted yield curve precede market tops, but it typically languishes beyond bear market bottoms. In January 2000, it was at a new all-time record high (and matched in May) and then fell off. Obviously that fact invited investors to watch that a peak was forming and to beware of the results that would follow. A bear market and recession did follow. And then in 2003, the valley caused by the terrorism high alert, war with Iraq, and other world events, was typically late, many months after the stock market's low. A bull market and economic expansion were already under way.

Housing Starts*

I place an asterisk on this "top" as its tops are not as clearly delineated and easy to see as the ones just discussed. It is evident that when housing starts top and head down, a recession *usually* follows. The obvious exception was the top to trough from 1964 to 1966, which did not identify a bona fide recession, merely a soft landing or, as some called it, a mild or growth recession. It did, however, point to the bear market from February 1966 until October 1966. The other obvious "miss" was the long-drawn-out decline from 1984 through 1991, which pointed to a recession for several years before one happened. But again, there were two brief but legitimate bear markets during that time frame, in 1987 and 1990. Other than those exceptions, recessions followed:

1. The *apparent* February 1959 peak, which preceded the recession starting in April 1960.
2. The January 1969 *obvious* peak preceded the recession starting in December of that year.
3. The January 1972 *obvious* peak preceded the recession starting in November of the following year.
4. The April 1978 *obvious* peak preceded the recession that started in January 1980.
5. The January 1981 *obvious* peak preceded the recession that started in July of that year.
6. The December 1998 *not-so-obvious* peak preceded the recession that started in March 2001. This decline from the peak was not of the magnitude of the others; it was the only decline that failed to drop at least 500,000 housing starts, and therefore it would likely not have been useful.

The January 2006 *obvious* peak pointed to a recession in 2007 or 2008. At the time of this writing, no recession had been confirmed by the NBER, so it was not yet clear whether this would be correct or yet another miss. Now you see why I put an asterisk on this indicator.

Unfortunately, the brief history and erratic behavior of this indicator make it only marginally dependable in forecasting recessions, but its *peaks have preceded the start of bear markets* by an average of 13.8 months. The lead time to recessions has been on average from 25 to 31 months, depending on how you count 1964 when there was no recession.

Perhaps housing starts real value as a leading indicator is in *identifying the coming economic recoveries that follow recessions.* Each of the "obvious" troughs bottom *before,* as happened in July 2000, or *during,* as in the other six recessions *but before the recession ends* (excluding the aforementioned 1966 bottom, which was not accompanied by recession). (See Figure 11.3.)

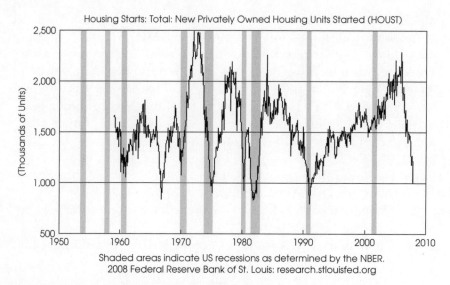

Figure 11.3 shows the shaded areas indicate US recessions as determined by the NBER.
2008 Federal Reserve Bank of St. Louis: research.stlouisfed.org

Figure 11.3   Housing Starts and Recessions
Source: U.S. Department of Commerce, Census Bureau

It is interesting to see in Table 11.6 that the start of the decline in housing starts precedes the start of the next bear market and recession. An increase in housing starts is a precursor to the end of the recession.

The rationale for the significance of housing starts on the economy has to do with the number of construction employees involved. Figure 11.4 shows the lagging increase of employees as housing starts increased from 2000 to 2006. That increase in employment contributed to the economic expansion of 2001 through 2007. You can readily see the lagging decrease following the building boom bust of 2006–2008.

The correlation of a declining employment in the construction area and recessions can be seen in Figure 11.5.

Other than the decrease of construction employment during World War II due to obvious reasons—the men were needed in the war effort—a recession has followed all leveling out and dips in construction employment almost immediately. The one dip in 1966–1967 that was not followed by an official recession was followed by a distinct slowing of the economy. Industrial production fell from the first quarter to the third quarter of 1967, and many argued that there was a growth recession in that year.

Table 11.6 Housing Starts and Their Relationship to Bear Markets and Recessions

Peak	Level	Trough	Level	Peak Lead to	Bear Start	End	Peak Lead to	Recession Start	Trough	Trough Lead to	Recession End
Feb-59	1667	Dec-60	1063	31	Dec-61	Jun-62	13	Apr-60	Dec-60	2	Feb-61
Feb-64	1820	Oct-66	843	24	Feb-66	Oct-66	n/a	none	Oct-66	n/a	n/a
Jan-69	1769	Jan-70	1085	−1	Dec-68	May-70	11	Dec-69	Jan-70	10	Nov-70
Jan-72	2494	Jan-75	904	12	Jan-73	Dec-74	22	Nov-73	Jan-75	2	Mar-75
Apr-78	2197	May-80	927	5	Sep-78	Apr-80	21	Jan-80	May-80	2	Jul-80
Jan-81	1547	Nov-81	837	3	Apr-81	Aug-82	6	Jul-81	Nov-81	12	Nov-82
Feb-84	2260	Jan-91	798	42	Aug-87 (Jul-90)	Oct-87 Oct-90)	77	Jul-90	Jan-91	2	Mar-91
Dec-98	1792	Jul-00	1465	−6	Jul-98	Aug-98	27	Mar-01	Jul-00	16	Nov-01
Jan-06	2265			21	Oct-07		23?	Dec-07?			

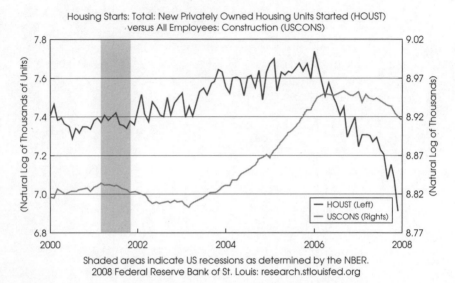

Figure 11.4   Housing Starts and Construction Employment
Source: Federal Reserve Bank of St. Louis

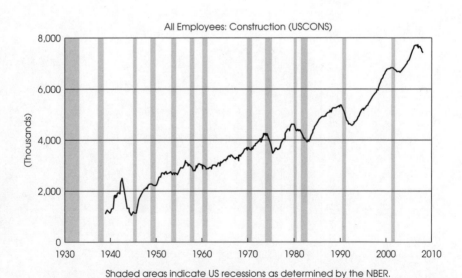

Figure 11.5   Construction Job Losses and Recession
Source: U.S. Department of Labor, Bureau of Labor Statistics

Lots of statistics and indicators are available for judging the state of the economy and the stock market, but I feel these are among the very best. When they are looked at in combination with the other indicators covered in this book, they should give you a good idea as to what to expect and how to invest. The next chapter covers other historic data that will help you put it all together when evaluating future situations.

CHAPTER 12

Bonus Indicators

In this chapter, we'll look at some interesting indicators that I have included in this book because you're unlikely to know about them otherwise. I'll also discuss that dreaded *r* word: recession. A widely held misconception is that it is defined as two successive quarters of negative gross national product, but that's not the "legal" description. As discussed in Chapter 6, the National Bureau of Economic Research defines a recession as a "significant decline in economic activity spread across the economy, lasting more than a few months, normally visible in real GDP, real income, employment, industrial production, and wholesale-retail sales." Further, they state that "a recession—the way we use the word—is a period of *diminishing* activity, rather than *diminished* activity." There are some little-known but accurate indicators for determining when recessions start and end. We do not have to wait, perhaps a year, for the NBER to pronounce the official dates after the fact.

The Single Best Day to Buy Each Year . . . Usually

Investing in January rather than December each year, *even if the amounts invested and returns are the same,* would result in some 8 percent greater ending value for the earlier investment. Usually the earlier you invest, with more time to grow, the better. By investing in January, you have an extra 11 months over investing in December and the market has a long-term upward bias. According to *Yahoo! Finance* and other sources: $4,000 per year over 30 years invested in December and earning 8 percent ends as $453,000 whereas investing in January of the same year and earning the same 8 percent ends as $489,000, a difference of $36,000, or about 8 percent more. That should be reason enough to get started early and stay the course.

Better yet would be to pick the low day of the year—lots of luck, you say? Actually, the Capitulation Indicator discussed in Chapter 8 does a pretty good job of that *at the end of bear markets.* The only problem is that there have only been 11 times over the last 50 years that it occurred, and that doesn't help to pinpoint the *annual* low each year. Most investors make annual (or more frequent) investments in their Individual Retirement Accounts or personal accounts and most would like to know what the single best day is to make that annual investment each year.

On January 24, 2005, I heard about an expert in Seasonal Affective Disorder from Cardiff University in Wales who had devised a formula that showed "that 24th January is *the worst day of the year.*" The psychologist was talking about a mental health issue relating to depression and did not have the American stock market in mind, and it sounded silly, but it got me thinking about whether it could have some relevance to the stock market. After all, the emotions of fear and greed play a big part in investing, as does enthusiasm and discouragement or depression. I was reminded of the January–February "gloom period" that prevailed at West Point when I was a cadet over 50 years ago, and for 150 years before that, and still today I would imagine.

Researching January 24 led me to discover that it had been the low for 1999, and was also within 3 percent of the lows in 1983, 1986, 1988, 1992, 1993, 1995, 1998, 2002, and 2006. Next I was surprised to discovered that since 1950, the *annual low occurred 23 times of the last 58* years *in January,* or **40 percent** of the time! No other month came close; only October with eight had more than three per month. One would think that any one day would have only a 1 in 250 (approximate number of trading days in a year) chance of being the low of the year, that is a 0.4 percent chance. But interestingly, the *first trading day of the new year was* the *low for the year nine times,* or nearly *16 percent of all annual lows. Slightly over one-half,* 31 of 58 or 53 percent, *were within 5* percent *of the lows, their average being within 1.4* percent*!* Seventy-seven percent of all the first trading days of January were within 4 percent of the lows, as a group average. All things considered, there can be no doubt that the single best day at or closest to the annual lows in the stock market is the first trading day of the year. Sometimes investing seems simple, doesn't it? See Table 12.1.

Table 12.1   January 2/3/4—The First Trading Day of the Year—The Single Best Day At or Closest to the Annual Lows

Dow Jones	1st Day	Annual Low	Date of Low	% Decline to Low
2008	13043.96			
2007	12474.50	12050.41	3-Mar	3.4%
2006	10847.41	10667.39	**20-Jan**	**1.7%**
2005	10729.43	10087.57	15-Apr	6.0%
2004	10409.85	9749.99	25-Oct	6.3%
2003	8607.52	7524.06	11-Mar	12.6%
2002	10073.40	7286.27	9-Oct	27.7%
2001	10646.15	8235.81	21-Sep	22.6%
2000	11357.51	9796.03	7-Mar	13.7%
1999	9184.27	9120.67	**22-Jan**	**0.7%**
1998	7965.04	7539.07	31-Aug	5.3%
1997	6442.49	6391.69	11-Apr	**0.8%**
1996	5177.45	5032.94	**10-Jan**	**2.8%**
1995	3838.48	3832.08	**30-Jan**	**0.2%**
1994	3756.60	3593.35	4-Apr	**4.3%**
1993	3309.22	3241.95	**20-Jan**	**2.0%**
1992	3172.41	3136.58	9-Oct	**1.1%**
1991	2610.64	2470.30	**9-Jan**	5.4%
1990	2810.15	2365.10	11-Oct	15.8%
1989	2144.64	2144.64	**3-Jan**	**0.0%**
1988	2015.25	1879.14	**20-Jan**	6.8%
1987	1927.31	1738.74	19-Oct	9.8%
1986	1537.73	1502.29	**22-Jan**	**2.3%**
1985	1198.87	1184.95	**4-Jan**	**1.2%**
1984	1252.74	1086.56	15-Jun	13.3%
1983	1027.05	1027.05	**3-Jan**	**0.0%**
1982	882.52	776.92	11-Aug	12.0%
1981	972.78	824.01	25-Sep	15.3%
1980	824.57	759.13	21-Apr	7.9%
1979	811.42	796.67	7-Nov	**1.8%**
1978	817.74	742.12	28-Feb	9.2%
1977	999.75	801.50	2-Nov	19.8%

(continued)

Table 12.1 *(continued)*

Dow Jones	1st Day	Annual Low	Date of Low	% Decline to Low
1976	858.71	858.71	**2-Jan**	**0.0%**
1975	632.04	632.04	**2-Jan**	**0.0%**
1974	855.32	577.60	6-Dec	32.5%
1973	1031.68	788.31	5-Dec	23.6%
1972	889.30	889.15	**26-Jan**	**0.0%**
1971	830.57	797.97	23-Nov	**3.9%**
1970	809.20	631.16	26-May	22.0%
1969	947.73	796.93	17-Dec	15.9%
1968	906.84	825.13	21-Mar	9.0%
1967	786.41	786.41	**3-Jan**	**0.0%**
1966	968.54	744.32	7-Oct	23.2%
1965	869.78	840.59	28-Jun	**3.4%**
1964	766.08	766.08	**2-Jan**	**0.0%**
1963	646.79	646.79	**2-Jan**	**0.0%**
1962	724.71	535.76	26-Jun	26.1%
1961	610.25	610.25	**3-Jan**	**0.0%**
1960	679.06	566.05	25-Oct	16.6%
1959	587.59	574.46	9-Feb	**2.2%**
1958	439.27	436.89	25-Feb	**0.5%**
1957	496.03	419.79	22-Oct	15.4%
1956	485.78	462.85	**23-Jan**	**4.7%**
1955	408.89	388.20	**17-Jan**	5.1%
1954	282.89	279.87	**11-Jan**	**1.1%**
1953	292.14	255.49	14-Sep	12.5%
1952	269.86	256.35	1-May	**5.0%**
1951	239.92	238.99	**2-Jan**	**0.4%**
1950	198.89	196.81	**13-Jan**	1.0%
Average decline to lows from the 1st day in January				**8.0%**

Your best option is to make your annual investment contribution on the first trading day of January each year, unless a bear market is under way; no bear market has *ever* ended in January. Actually, over the last 100-plus years, every other month has been the low for one or more bear markets with October having witnessed the most, with six—but none in January. So what to do?

If the market is in a bona fide bear market, as defined as down at least 16 percent on both the Dow Jones Industrials *and* the Standard & Poor's 500 Index, it would be wise to wait and watch for capitulation or a buy signal from either the Dow Theory or the Schannep Timing Indicator. Capitulation has been identified at or within three days of the bear market lows 8 of the last 12 bear market bottoms. On those occasions it certainly would have been wise to use that as the trigger for your annual investment in those years.

The Composite Indicator, which will be covered in Chapter 13, takes into consideration the status of capitulation, the Dow Theory, the Schannep Timing Indicator, and the definitions of bull and bear. Therefore, its recommended investment stance is the one to follow on the first of each year. Table 12.2 shows that investing between 50 and 100 percent on the first trading day of each year has been appropriate most of the time. But it was appropriate *not* to take an initial position in 1958, 1974, 1978, 1979, 1980 and 1982—only 6 of the last 56 years—because of a zero percent investment position dictated by the Composite Indicator. Later in those years a signal was given to invest that beat a buy-and-hold strategy in 1974, 1978, and 1980. No signal was given in 1979; that year it was more profitable to stay out of the market and collect 11 percent interest in money market funds! For 2008, I had advised not to buy on the first trading day as the Composite Indicator was inching toward a sell, which came in January. Over the long term, *the strategy of timing and/or adjusting the amount of investment on the first trading day of a new year in accordance with the status of the Composite has resulted in doubling the results of a simple buy-and-hold strategy.* That's the difference between earning **12.7 or 11.1 percent** annually. You make the choice, but either way, investing some or all on the first trading day of each new year usually works pretty well. Details are shown in Table 12.2.

January's Good, February's Better; Both Are Best as Indicators

Much has been written about the first day, the first five days, and the whole month of January being predictive of the rest of the year. It's often paraphrased "As goes January, so goes the year." When the "January Barometer" as devised by Yale Hirsch in 1972 is an up month, the chances of that year closing higher than January's month-end have been 84.6 percent. With February, the percentage goes up to

Table 12.2   Using the Composite Signal on the First Trading Day

Dow Jones	Composite Timed 1st Buy	Composite Results For Year	Buy & Hold (B&H) Results	Year-End Dow Jones	Year-End Yield	$100 in 1954 Grows to Timed	$100 in 1954 Grows to B&H
2008							
2007	12474.50	5.4%	6.3%	13264.82	2.3%	$54,586	$28,694
2006	10847.41	10.6%	14.9%	12463.15	2.3%	$50,683	$26,422
2005	10729.43	−0.1%	−0.6%	10717.50	2.3%	$44,892	$22,544
2004	9749.99	4.0%	5.3%	10783.01	2.2%	$43,926	$22,167
2003	8607.52	23.0%	28.3%	10453.92	2.0%	$42,236	$21,042
2002	10073.40	−6.5%	−15.0%	8341.63	2.3%	$34,339	$16,401
2001	10646.15	−7.0%	−5.4%	10021.50	2.0%	$36,726	$19,295
2000	11357.51	−4.5%	−4.5%	10786.85	1.7%	$39,490	$20,396
1999	9184.27	20.9%	26.7%	11497.12	1.5%	$41,351	$21,352
1998	7965.04	17.9%	17.8%	9181.43	1.7%	$34,202	$16,850
1997	6442.49	24.4%	24.4%	7908.25	1.8%	$29,010	$14,304
1996	5177.45	28.0%	28.0%	6448.27	2.0%	$23,320	$11,494
1995	3838.48	34.5%	35.8%	5117.12	2.3%	$18,219	$8,979
1994	3593.35	4.5%	4.8%	3834.44	2.7%	$13,545	$6,614
1993	3241.95	16.4%	16.4%	3754.09	2.7%	$12,962	$6,309
1992	3136.58	7.3%	7.3%	3301.11	3.1%	$11,136	$5,419
1991	2610.64	22.4%	23.3%	3168.83	3.0%	$10,378	$5,052

Year							
1990	2810.15	−0.7%	−0.4%	2633.66	3.9%	$8,479	$4,096
1989	2144.64	27.8%	30.7%	2753.20	3.7%	$8,539	$4,114
1988	2015.25	12.7%	15.5%	2168.57	3.7%	$6,681	$3,149
1987	1927.31	37.8%	6.0%	1938.83	3.7%	$5,928	$2,725
1986	1537.73	26.1%	26.1%	1895.95	3.5%	$4,302	$2,572
1985	1198.87	31.7%	31.7%	1546.67	4.0%	$3,412	$2,040
1984	1252.74	−5.5%	1.3%	1211.56	5.0%	$2,591	$1,549
1983	1027.05	24.8%	24.8%	1258.64	4.5%	$2,741	$1,530
1982	891.17	24.3%	24.8%	1046.55	5.2%	$2,197	$1,226
1981	972.78	4.4%	−2.8%	875.00	6.4%	$1,767	$983
1980	844.80	24.0%	20.5%	963.99	5.6%	$1,693	$1,011
1979	n/a	11.0%	10.3%	838.74	6.1%	$1,365	$839
1978	810.12	9.4%	2.9%	805.01	6.0%	$1,230	$761
1977	999.75	−10.8%	−11.8%	831.17	5.5%	$1,124	$740
1976	858.71	22.0%	22.0%	1004.63	4.1%	$1,260	$838
1975	632.04	42.7%	42.7%	852.41	4.4%	$1,033	$687
1974	666.07	1.1%	−21.5%	616.24	6.1%	$724	$482
1973	1031.68	−15.5%	−12.4%	850.86	4.2%	$716	$613
1972	889.30	16.5%	17.8%	1020.02	3.2%	$847	$700
1971	830.57	9.0%	9.6%	890.20	3.5%	$727	$594
1970	809.20	12.5%	8.6%	838.92	3.8%	$667	$542
1969	947.73	−6.0%	−11.0%	800.36	4.2%	$593	$499
1968	906.84	4.2%	7.6%	943.75	3.3%	$631	$561
1967	786.41	17.3%	18.5%	905.11	3.3%	$606	$521
1966	968.54	−2.1%	−14.8%	785.69	4.1%	$516	$440

(continued)

Table 12.2 (continued)

Dow Jones	Composite Timed 1st Buy	Composite Results For Year	Buy & Hold (B&H) Results	Year-End Dow Jones	Year-End Yield	$100 in 1954 Grows to Timed	$100 in 1954 Grows to B&H
1965	869.78	13.9%	13.9%	969.26	3.0%	$527	$517
1964	766.08	18.2%	18.2%	874.13	3.6%	$463	$454
1963	646.79	20.1%	20.1%	762.95	3.1%	$392	$384
1962	724.71	5.2%	-7.2%	652.10	3.6%	$326	$320
1961	610.25	21.8%	21.8%	731.14	3.1%	$310	$344
1960	679.06	-7.6%	-5.8%	615.89	3.5%	$255	$283
1959	587.59	17.1%	19.5%	679.36	3.1%	$275	$300
1958	460.34	27.7%	37.4%	583.65	3.4%	$235	$251
1957	496.03	-6.0%	-7.8%	435.69	5.0%	$184	$183
1956	485.78	7.5%	6.9%	499.47	4.6%	$196	$198
1955	408.89	25.2%	25.2%	488.40	4.4%	$182	$186
1954	289.34	45.6%	48.3%	404.39	4.3%	$146	$148
1953	Composite Timing Indicator data began 1954					$100	$100

87 percent. Unfortunately, February is as likely to close down as up, with 31 down months and 31 up since 1945. When February has declined, the chances of the market ending higher by year-end is only 57 percent; for January the figure is 54 percent. But the absolute best predictive record over the last 60 years is when *both close up in the same year*, in which case the S&P 500 has closed the year higher than February month-end 22 of the 23 times, a 95.7 percentage. When both close down, which only occurred 14 times, the chances of an up year drop to 43 percent; that is, there is a 57 percent chance of a down year. I'm not sure why this kind of historical phenomenon repeats itself, but the odds are too good to keep to myself, so make of it what you will.

A "Typical" Year

Mark Twain is said to have commented on the stock market: "October. This is one of the peculiarly dangerous months to speculate in stocks. The others are July, January, September, April, November, May, March, June, December, August and February." If there is such a thing as a typical year, the stock market would look something like Figure 12.1. This chart was kindly provided by CXO Advisory and printed with their permission. Other periods of time show the same general pattern. Although this may be a case of

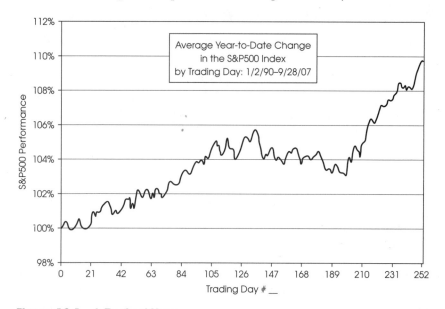

Figure 12.1   A Typical Year

statistics not lying, they certainly don't look like there's ever been such a thing as a down year, and we know they do occur every four years or so. More on that in the next section.

An old Wall Street adage says to "sell in May and go away," although that may be a bit early as the midyear setback typically lasts from July through October. A whole cottage industry has grown up around how best to invest using this pattern. Yale Hirsch created this strategy in 1986 and has calculated what selling on April 30 and then buying back on October 31 would do for investment results. His *Stock Trader's Almanac* shows that $10,000 invested on each April 30 starting in 1950 and sold on the next October 31 grew to just $10,341 by October of 2002 whereas $10,000 invested on each October 31 and sold on the next May 1 rose to $588,413. Sy Harding in *Riding the Bear* expanded on the "Best Six Months" strategy using Gerald Appel's Moving Average Convergence Divergence (MACD). The backtested switches nearly tripled the results. For a more thorough explanation, see Harding's book or *All About Market Timing* by Les Masonson. Another strategy shown there avoids September entirely but uses other months to initiate investments. There are a lot of variations on just this one theme of the typical annual pattern. I'll leave it to you to determine if any are for you.

What about Any Current Year?

A well-known repetitious pattern is the "presidential cycle" consisting of the four years from pre-election, to election, to postelection, to the midterm election years. There has been a tendency for the midterm years to be accompanied by bear market lows, as shown in Table 12.3.

As a matter of interest, the pre-election year has gone up some 81 percent of the time and averaged a +12.2 percent gain. The election year has risen some 78 percent of the time and averaged +9.5 percent.

Table 12.3   Stock Market's Four-Year Cycle

4-Year Cycle	1950	1954	1958	1962	1966	1970	1974	
Bear Market Lows	6/49	Not	10/57	6/62	10/66	5/70	12/74	
4-Year Cycle	1978	1982	1986	1990	1994	1998	2002	2006
Bear Market Lows	2/78 also 8/80	8/82	10/87	10/90	Not	8/98 also 9/01	10/02	Not

The postelection has risen 56 percent of the time and averaged +3.4 percent, and the midyear election year has risen 58 percent of the time by an average of +3.6 percent, according to data from Ned Davis Research.

What I have found most interesting about the presidential cycle is that the year in question is often forecast by the trend at the close of the preceding year. Since 1903 the trend at the previous *midterm* (*1906*) year-end has pointed to the new *pre-election* (*1907*) *years* gain or loss some **88 percent** of the time. In other words, had the market topped in 2006 and started into a bear market, then the odds favored that 2007 would be a down year. However, with the bull market still intact at 2006 year-end, the odds favored that 2007 would be an up year. Interesting, eh? Unfortunately, *midterm* election-year results such as in 2006 are not similarly predicted by the prior *postelection* year-end direction. The odds are only 54 to 46 percent that the 2005 year-end uptrend will point to 2006's result, so the presidential cycle itself is not the reason for expecting an up year. Incidentally, the *pre-election* (*2007*) year-end trend is 85 percent correct in pointing to the *election* (*2008*) year's result, and the *election* year-end trend is 70 percent correct in pointing to the *postelection* (*2009*) year's result. These figures were determined by comparing each of the presidential cycle years with the history of "Bull and Bear Markets of the Twentieth and Twenty-First Centuries" in Chapter 7.

Let me remind you that these and other percentages shown elsewhere may be impressive, but they are not 100 percent. In other words, even with the odds in your favor, the result is not preordained. There are lots of cycles in the stock market and lots of believers in one or the other of them. Personally, the only ones I *count on* are the business cycle and the tides that are evident in the ocean *and* the stock market—the bull-bear market cycle.

How to Tell What the Next Year Will Bring (If the Market Has Just Sustained a Multiple-Year Decline)

Table 12.4 looks like a classic bell curve. Two-thirds of the time the market rises on an inflation-adjusted basis (i.e. *rises in excess of the inflation rate*). A majority of years the stock market rises between 0 and 30 percent. There are a few extremes when it has risen over +50 percent and some that have declined over −30 percent. But beyond the impression that the stock market is a pretty good place to be over the long term, what does it tell us about the near term?

There are a number of times that the market declines over a multiple-year time frame, which are shown at the bottom of Table 12.4. What becomes apparent is *the aftermath* of those declines. Usually the first year after such a decline, you will see the market advances

Table 12.4   82-Year Return History for Common Stocks (Adjusted for Inflation) 1926–2007, Average Annual Compounded Real Return = 7%

Up years 56 68.3%
Down years 26 31.7%

-40%	-30%	-20%	-10%	0%	+10%	+20%	+30%	+40%	+50%	+60%
					2006					
					1999					
					1996					
					1988					
					1986					
					1983					
				2007	1982					
				2005	1980					
				2004	1976	2003				
		2001		1993	1972	1998				
		2000	1994	1992	1971	1991				
		1981	1990	1987	1965	1989	1997			
		1977	1978	1984	1964	1975	1995			
		1969	1970	1979	1959	1967	1985			
		1966	1962	1968	1952	1963	1955			
	2002	1957	1960	1956	1951	1961	1945			
1974	1973	1941	1953	1948	1944	1950	1938	1958		
1937	1946	1940	1947	1939	1942	1949	1936	1935		1954
1931	1930	1929	1934	1932	1926	1943	1927	1928	1933	

Rates of Real Return (%)

*Returns based on the S&P 500 adjusted for inflation.
Source: Ron Surz, *The Monitor* (January 2005) by, Investment Management Consultant Association. Printed with permission.

All Multiple Down Years	Have Always Been Followed by Multiple Up Years
1929–1930–1931	1932*–1933
1940–1941	1942–1943–1944–1945
1946–1947	1948–1949–1950–1951–1952
1969–1970†	1971–1972
1973–1974	1975–1976
1977–1978†	1979–1980
2000–2001–2002	2003–2004–2005–2006–2007

*1932 was a down year but trailed deflation.
†1970 and 1978 were actually up slightly but trailed inflation.

modestly with only two particularly strong years: 1975 and 2003 (up +25 percent). The other five times the increase was between 0 and +20 percent, inflation adjusted. But the **most important historic precedent is that after** *each* **of the multiple-year declines (inflation adjusted), the market has** *always* **had** *multiple-year advances.* **That meant that 2003 would be the start of a multiple-year advance, and indeed it was.**

About Recessions

The National Bureau of Economic Research (NBER), the nonprofit organization that is the government's official arbiter of when recessions begin and end, bases its assessment on numerous economic indicators as described in Chapter 6. One thing that all recessions have had in common is that total nonfarm payroll dropped from the previous year. The Business Cycle Dating Committee of the NBER has not specified that as a requirement in their definition, but nonetheless it has been a constant in past recessions.

How to Know When One Is Coming

As you know from Chapter 11, there are leading advance warnings about upcoming bear markets and recessions. The first of what I call "Three Tops and a Tumble" is a volume top where New York Stock Exchange (NYSE) monthly volume tends to peak some five or six months before the stock market itself does. The bear markets that follow, in turn, tend to "predict" and be followed by recessions nearly three-quarters of the time since the turn of the *last* century. Another top is when the *yield curve* reaches a ratio of .95 percent of the three-month Treasury bill rate monthly average divided by the 10-year Treasury bond yield, in which case a bear market follows in six to seven months and a recession six to seven months after that. Yet another top to be followed by bear markets and recessions is *consumer confidence.* Since 1967, *each* high point has been followed by a bear market five months later, on average, *and* a recession eight months after that. Those three tops pointed out early in the year 2000 that the bear market and recession were coming and pointed to the start of the recession between January and August of 2001. In November 2001, the NBER announced it "officially" had started in March 2001. In 2007, these indicators were similar to their alignment in 2000.

Why Care If One Is Coming?

If you're a businessperson, you'll want to know if a recession is coming so as to adjust your business plan regarding inventory, hiring, and cost control in light of probable lower sales and profits. The larger the business, the larger the impact. It is said that Lee Iacocca, when he headed Chrysler, told his chief economist "to just let him know six months before the next recession." Obviously that is easier said than done. I am told that the "forecasters' handbook" lists rule number one as "Never, EVER, forecast a recession." This is due partly to the fact that it is difficult to do, and then of course nobody likes the messenger who brings bad news. *As an investor, you will want to know when a recession is coming because in almost all cases a bear market will precede a recession. Of the 21 recessions in the twenty and twenty-first centuries, only 4 were not preceded or accompanied by a bear market.*

How to Know If One Is Occurring

A rising unemployment rate can be one way of knowing that a recession is occurring. The White House Council of Economic Advisers annual report released on January 12, 2001 stated that the economy would avoid a recession. However, on March 1, 2001, I said that a mild recession looks like a done deal. At that time, 95 percent of American economists said there would not be a recession, according to *The Economist* (March 2005). The Economic Cycle Research Institute (ECRI) was one of the very few forecasters with whom I am familiar also forecasting in March 2001 that there would be a recession. Even in April 2001, the Conference Board said, "No recession is on the horizon." Actually . . . one had already started in March. When the unemployment rate has upticked and looks like it is starting to rise, what are the implications? Not much if it only rises a tenth or two of a percent, but it is significant if it moves much farther than that. The *Wall Street Journal* wrote on August 11, 2000, that the Federal Reserve has never been able to allow unemployment to rise by more than three-tenths of 1 percent without causing a recession. *Unfortunately, it is not that simple, nor is it true,* because no recession followed a *four*-tenth rise on numerous occasions (1951, 1963, 1967, 1976, 1986, and 1995). *But there is a definite relationship between a rising unemployment rate and a recession and a bear market.*

On **11** occasions since 1948, when the Bureau of Labor Statistics data on the civilian labor force unemployment rate began, the level has **risen four-tenths of a percentage point** *on a three-month moving average basis* from the *cyclical low three-month average.* **On *all* 10 of those occasions prior to the most recent one in January, 2008, a recession was just starting or was about to begin, and 8 of the 10 were accompanied by bear markets**. There have only been 10 previous times that the moving average rose four-tenths, and only 10 recessions in that time, so *this indicator caught them all.* If the NBER proclaims that a recession has occurred in 2008, then the record goes to 11 out of 11.

In 2000, the three-month average of 3.9 in both September and October and 4.0 for November was 3.933. The record would indicate that, if that was the low for the cycle and it rose to **4.333** *as an average of a future three-month period,* a recession would occur and a bear market would probably also occur. It was particularly timely to be aware of this phenomenon because the *Wall Street Journal* (1/2/01) Forecasting Survey for 2001 showed the average estimate of 54 economists for unemployment for May of 2001 to be **4.4 percent**! On May 4, 2001, the April figure was reported as 4.5, which when combined with February's 4.2 and March's 4.3 averaged 4.333; hence a recession was forecast! At that time, the Dow Jones level was 10,951. Much later, the NBER announced the recession had begun that March.

The bear market low four and a half months later, on September 21, 2001, was 8,235. Then on November 26, 2001, with the Dow Jones at 9982.75, the NBER proclaimed the recession officially *began* in March of 2001. The recession was ending *that very month,* but the NBER would not make that determination until July 2003! The post 9/11 bull market turned out to be a mini–bull market, lasting only six months and rising just 29 percent on the Dow Industrials. It was an "official" bull market, although a disappointing one, before returning to a bear market, which ended October 9, 2002, at a low of 7,286.27.

In 2008 a similar thing occurred. The lowest three-month average was 4.43 percent form late 2006. October and November, 2007 had originally been reported as 4.7 percent each. At that point I wrote "2008 does look like a recessionary year which may actually be dated to this quarter of this year (4th quarter of 2007)." Then on January 4th, 2008, the Bureau of Labor Statistics reported a change for October to 4.8 percent and the number for December as 5.0 percent; therefore the three-month average became 4.83 percent. That four-tenths of a percentage point meant a recession was forecast. At that time, the Dow Jones level was 12,800. That is when I advised subscribers to my market letter that "A recession is no longer approaching . . . it is here now." When the NBER gets around to determining when it started, I would guess they will say either December of 2007 or January 2008.

Obviously, four-tenths is a larger percentage from 4.0 to 4.4 than it would be from 6.0 to 6.4; however, four-tenths continues to be the figure that works regardless of the unemployment level. When the four-tenth-point rise occurs, the market will usually already be in a bear market, so *it is not a leading indicator.* A further decline of nearly 14 percent by the stock market has been the average of the 10 previous times, even including the two times when no bear market resulted. A further decline of nearly 16 percent was the average during bear markets. Only once has the four-tenth percent signal *preceded* a recession; once it coincided with the start; and the other eight times it lagged the start of recession by one to four months. Bear in mind that the NBER usually does not identify recessions until many months, even a year or more after they start (or end), so this four-tenth percent indicator *beats them to the punch every time.*

Table 12.5 shows the rising unemployement rate sell indicator. As you can see, a rise of +.four-tenths percent (*on a three-month rolling average basis*) in the unemployment rate has resulted in recessions all 10 previous times and has been accompanied by 8 bear markets.

It is obvious from Table 12.5 that by the time of the four-tenth percent rise (on a three-month average basis), the **recession is probably already under way but not yet identified as "official"** by the NBER. Nine of the 10 times this indicator lagged or was coincident with the start of the recession.

Another excellent indicator came into being in 1968 and was the earliest to pinpoint the last six recessions. The *Survey of Professional Forecasters,* the so-called Anxious Index (see Figure 12.2), is the oldest quarterly survey of macroeconomic forecasts in the United States, according to the Federal Reserve Bank of Philadelphia, which took over the survey in 1990 from the American Statistical Association and the NBER. The six times when one-third of the economists in the survey predict a recession in the following quarter, a recession has indeed occurred. And a bear market was already under way all six times! This indicator gave a signal in February 2001, the month before that recession's actual start, and most recently in

Table 12.5 Rising Unemployment Rate "Sell" Indicator

Bull Market High	Dow Jones Level	3-Month +.4 rise "SELL"	DJIA Date of Release*	Lags Recession (Months)	Recession Start	Bear Market Low	Dow Jones Low Level	Further Drop from .4 to Lows
5/46	212.50	Jan-49	177.92	2 lag	Nov-48	Jun-49	161.60	9.2%
1/53	293.79	Nov-53	282.71	4 lag	Jul-53	Nov-53†	273.88	3.1%
4/56	521.05	Sep-57	461.70	1 lag	Aug-57	Oct-57	419.79	9.1%
1/60	685.47	Oct-59	650.92	6 lead	Apr-60	Oct-60†	596.07	8.4%
12/68	985.21	Feb-70	784.12	2 lag	Dec-69	May-70	631.16	19.5%
1/73	1051.70	Mar-74	847.54	4 lag	Nov-73	Dec-74	577.60	31.8%
9/78	907.74	Jan-80	881.48	0	Jan-80	Apr-80	759.13	13.9%
4/81	1024.05	Nov-81	892.69	4 lag	Jul-81	Aug-82	776.92	13.0%
7/90	2999.75	Sep-90	2510.64	2 lag	Jul-90	Oct-90	2365.10	5.8%
1/00	11,722.98	Apr-01	10,951.24	1 lag	Mar-01	Sep-01	8235.81	24.8%
10/07	14,164.53	Dec-07	12,800.18	0?	Dec-07?			
		Average lag :		**1.2-month**		**Average further drop:**		**13.8%**

*First Friday of month following the month reported on.
†Low if no actual bear market (otherwise shown).

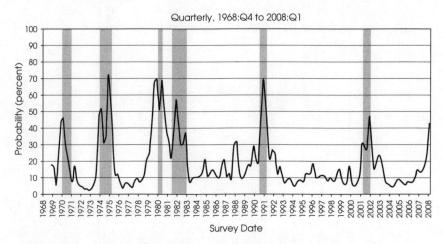

Quarterly, 1968:Q4 to 2008:Q1

Survey Date

Figure 12.2   The Anxious Index: Probability of Decline in Real Gross Domestic Product in the Following Quarter

February 2008. The average *lead time to recession* is one and a half months, and the further drop to the bear market lows averaged 20 percent. The data, released around the 15th of the middle month of each quarter, can be found at www.philadelphiafed.org/files/spf/anxind.html.

These two indicators, the Anxious Index and the Rising Unemployment Rate indicator, are impressive—and between them are the best I know of for determining when recessions start.

Bull Markets Begin during Recessions

The good news about recessions is that bull markets begin in their midst. Only one of the 21 bull markets in the twenty-first century started outside of the recession period, as can be seen in Chapter 5. The continued rise in unemployment pointed to the bear market's end and the bull market's start when it rose a full 1 percent by August 2001 as reported on September 7, just two weeks before the lows on September 21 (See Table 12.6). As further evidence of the importance of a four-tenth-point rise in unemployment as described earlier, *the unemployment rate has gone on to rise 1 full percent from the low on each of the 10 previous times* after such a four-tenth-percent rise occurred. Surprisingly, no bear market accompanied those full 1 percent rises in 1953 or 1960, but bear markets did coincide the

Table 12.6 Rising Unemployment Rate "Buy" Indicator

Full +1.0 Rise Buy	Dow Jones Date of Release*	% Buy Above the Low	Bear Market Low	Dow Jones Low Level	Bull Market High	Dow Jones High Level	% Rise from +1 to High
Feb-49	174.93	8.2%	Jun-49	161.60	Apr-56	521.05	197.9%
Nov-53	281.51	2.8%	Nov-53†	273.88	Apr-56	521.05	85.1%
Nov-57	447.20	6.5%	Oct-57	419.79	Dec-61	734.91	64.3%
Oct-60	596.07	0.0%	Oct-60†	596.07	Dec-61	734.91	23.3%
Mar-70	791.84	25.5%	May-70	631.16	Jan-73	1051.70	32.8%
Sep-74	584.56	1.2%	Dec-74	577.60	Sep-76	1014.79	73.6%
Apr-80	810.92	6.8%	Apr-80	759.13	Apr-81	1024.05	26.3%
Nov-81	892.69	14.9%	Aug-82	776.92	Aug-87	2722.42	205.0%
Nov-90	2590.10	9.5%	Oct-90	2365.10	Jul-98	9337.97	260.5%
Aug-01	9605.85	14.3%	Sep-01	8235.81	Mar-02	10635.25	10.7%
Ave lead 1 month		**Above low: 8.9%**					**Ave. gain: 97.9%**

*First Friday of month following the month reported on.
†Recent low if no actual bear market (otherwise shown).

other eight times. Even as the unemployment rate continued to rise to a full 2 percent increase as the recessions deepened, the stock market, as it usually does, began to anticipate the turnaround in the economy and turned up. **The 1 percent rise has therefore become the "darkness before the dawn." It turns out to be an excellent buy signal pointing to the start of bull markets**. The 1 percent "indicator" has occurred *within an average of 9* percent of *the bear market low* point, and the *subsequent rise after the signal has exceeded 100* percent. (Thanks to Kenneth L. Fisher for originally writing about this phenomenon in his *Wall Street Waltz*.)

How to Know When Recessions Will End

Bull markets are, of course, leading indicators of economic expansion, as shown in Table 5.3 in Chapter 5, "Stock Market as a Business Cycle Predictor." In the twentieth century, *every* bull market was accompanied or followed shortly by economic expansions. Recessions ended some four months on average after bull markets started. In 2002, that pointed to January–February. The average length of recessions since the depression has been ten and a quarter months, also pointing to January–February 2002. Nine of the last 11 recessions ended in less than a year, again pointing to January–February 2002. But those are historical averages. Is there a better way of knowing without waiting for the NBER to announce 21 months later that the recession ended in November of 2001? Fortunately, there is something about capacity utilization and total non-farm payroll that tells us when a recession is over. (See Figure 12.3.)

When industries are in recession, they typically use less of their factory's capacity to produce their reduced output than when in an expansionary phase. The change from a declining rate to an increasing rate defines a trough. The Federal Reserve has reported Capacity Utilization since 1967, and Non-Farm Payrolls (all employees in non-farm jobs) since 1939. In the case of non-farm payrolls, the trough is based on the decline from the prior year's level reversing in magnitude in the month shown. My thanks to Jonathan Stein for the chart and bringing the non-farm relationship to my attention. As you can see in Table 12.7, the decline in capacity utilization and the change for non-farm payrolls has ended at or near the month that recessions have ended. Therefore, when the following months show gains, that

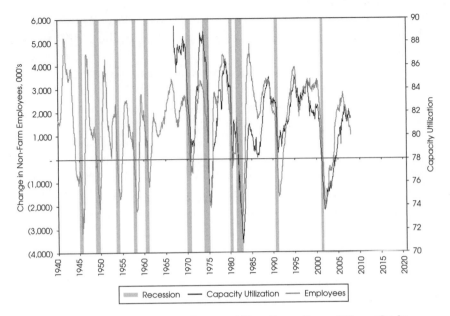

Figure 12.3   Capacity Utilization and Non-Farm Payroll Troughs in Relation to Recessions Ending

Table 12.7   When Recessions End

Capacity Utilization Trough	Non-Farm Employee Trough	Recession Ending Month	Cap. Util Trough lead(−) or lag(+) to Recession's End	Empl. Trough lead(−) or lag(+) to Recession's End
n/a	Sep-45	Oct-45	n/a	−1
n/a	Oct-49	Oct-49	n/a	0
n/a	Jul-54	May-54	n/a	+2
n/a	May-58	Apr-58	n/a	+1
n/a	Apr-61	Feb-61	n/a	+2
Nov-70	Nov-70	Nov-70	0	0
Mar-75	Jun-75	Mar-75	0	+3
Jul-80	Jul-80	Jul-80	0	0
Dec-82	Oct-82	Nov-82	+1	−1
Mar-91	May-91	Mar-91	0	+2
Dec-02	Feb-02	Nov-01	+1	+3

identifies that the low point of the trough is in place. Thus you can tell that the recession is over many months before the NBER makes its announcement.

Since 1967, when the Federal Reserve began reporting capacity utilization, there have been six recessions, as shown in Figure 12.3. In *each* of the previous recessions, there was a trough in the capacity utilization index that bottomed coincident with the recession's end. In 1970, 1975, 1980, and 1991, *the* low month for capacity utilization was the month that the recession ended. In 1982 and 2001, it was one month later. Note there was a bit of a trough in 1986, but since there was no recession, there was nothing to announce. This index is reported midmonth for the prior month so you can see in midmonth if the level is lower than the previously reported month. The record for non-farm payrolls goes even further back and its record of making a trough just as recessions end is every bit as impressive. The first increase will identify the prior month as having ended the recession! The thing about recessions is that they always end, and for the last 40 years capacity utilization, and for the last nearly 70 years non-farm payrolls, have told *when* they ended.

As previously discussed, housing starts also tend to trough during recessions. Since 1959, there have been seven obvious troughs, which signaled the end was near for six recessions. So there's something else to keep an eye on when watching for a recession to end.

Now that we have the economy all figured out (we do, don't we?), let's get back to the stock market. I am reminded of a meeting I attended years ago where a well-known economist was talking about the positive outlook for the economy. When he was asked what the implications were for the stock market, his answer was "Who knows, I'm talking economics here." No, the stock market and the economy are not inextricably linked. Most times they are, but not always.

A recession can, and has, occurred without a bear market preceding it, and a bull market can, and has, proceeded even with a recession occurring in its midst. But it's the stock market that we're most interested in, and making money, so let's move on to the next chapter and look at a most exciting way to use our indicators.

PART V

THE EPITOME
OF SYNERGY

13

The All-Inclusive Composite Indicator

I t is time to put all that we know about the Dow Theory for the twenty-first century, capitulation, the Schannep Timing Indicator, and the definitions of bull and bear and their aftermath results in the stock market all together into a Composite Indicator for timing the stock market. In this chapter, you will see that combining these indicators provides results that are better than those of the component parts.

Composite Timing Indicator: The Epitome of Synergy

I have believed for many years that the Dow Theory and my Schannep Timing Indicator are the two premier stock market major trend timing indicators with *documented and verified* long-term records that set the standard for market timing. At the same time, I have been concerned that both are *sometimes* slow in determining a change in the market's trend. Obviously, no indicator can pick market tops and bottoms precisely. None has come closer on a consistent basis than these two, yet there is always room for improvement. By combining the two and adding some other tried and true indicators, I believe that real synergism has been attained. Synergy: "The interaction of two or more agents or forces so that *their combined effect is greater than the sum of their individual effects.*"

I have referred to certain "pre-buy conditions" in my writings since 1976 and have informally incorporated them with my indicator in a successful effort to improve its results. The most continuously successful such indicator has been capitulation. When bear markets end in an identifiable capitulation, that is clearly the time to start buying. It is usually the first indication of a turn in the tide, followed later by the Dow Theory and/or the Schannep Timing Indicator, and finally the definition of a bull market is met.

As you will see, with this Composite Indicator, I buy 50 percent of my intended investment position when capitulation occurs and wait for confirmation from one of the other indicators to complete to a 100 percent investment posture. The definition of a bull market is typically the last indicator to come into play. A person usually is fully invested by that time, but if not, that is the time to get fully invested. The definition of bull and bear markets can come into play because, after all, with the odds of markets going significantly farther after meeting the definition being as good as we have determined them to be, then those definitions should figure into the buy or sell Decision.

"Spiders" (SPY—Standard & Poor's Depositary Receipts), "Diamonds" (DIA—Dow Jones Index Shares), and the New York Stock Exchange (NYSE) Composite iShares (NYC) are the most appropriate investment vehicles to assure results consistent with the stock market's behavior.

Putting it all together in a *Combined Indicator* has resulted in the best of all worlds, a Composite Timing Indicator that performs in *total* better than *any* of the individual parts. The 50-plus-year record shows a total annual average increase of just over 15 percent, considerably better than the results of buying and holding, which are typically about 10 percent. A 15 percent annual return results in a doubling of an investment in just under 5 years, quadrupling in just under 10 years, and on and on. The 10 percent average for buying and holding results in a doubling in just over 7 years, as you may know from the "rule of 72," which shows the time to double an investment by dividing 72 by the compound growth rate.

This is probably an appropriate time to point out that the historical record that follows is not a live record for several reasons: The statistics I use in the Schannep Timing Indicator were not available until 1968. Money market funds, which are used whenever a sell signal is in effect, were not invented until 1972. The first index fund was not introduced until 1976, and I was not able to produce *daily* calculations used in the capitulation and the Schannep Timing Indicators until 1984. Finally, the vehicles that I suggest be used, Spiders and Diamonds, were not available until 1993 and 1998 respectively, and the NYSE iShares not until 2004. While I believe the calculations are correct, it is probably prudent to disclaim perfection. In any event, the overall result is impressive.

While the Composite Timing Indicator is new, its components have existed for years. The underlying Dow Theory was first postulated over 100 years ago, and my own Schannep Timing Indicator was first formulated 40 years ago. The Composite Timing Indicator is just *formally incorporated* from the various components that were uncovered over many previous years. As you know, beating the stock market is an ongoing *Battle for Investment Survival*, to use the name of an excellent book on the subject with that title, by Gerald M. Loeb. This Composite Timing Indicator is the end result of a lifetime of work with the stock market, but there may be room for improvement. After all, anything having to do with timing the stock market has to be considered a work in progress. Whether you are a subscriber to my Market Letter or purchaser of this book, you are entitled to the best I can offer, and I feel that the Composite Timing Indicator is just that.

Specific Details of the Composite Timing Indicator

When any one of the four possible buy or one of the three possible sell indicators occurs, you should follow it by committing **one-half** of your intended investment position, either to investing or to selling, as the case may be.

The first type of the buy signal is typically the capitulation indicator. Different technicians use various indicators as shown in Chapter 8 to determine capitulation. I use short-term oscillators on the three major market indices. When the negative values for each reach their *specific* levels, it is an indication of capitulation. Such levels have been attained on only 11 occasions during the last 50 years. This indicator has appeared on average within 3.2 percent of the market lows in the bear market years of 1962, 1970, 1974, 1987, 1990, 1998, 2001, and 2002. On three occasions there was a double capitulation during the same bear market bottoming process. When that happens, you can count that as a follow-on buy signal but only increase your commitment to a 75 percent invested position.

As you know from the discussion of capitulation, it can occur only at or near bear market lows and does not occur at or near bull market highs, so is not also a sell indicator.

The second and third types of buy signals can also be sell indicators; they are the Dow Theory and the Schannep Timing Indicator. In the complete record that follows, I have used the original Dow Theory during the twentieth century portion of the record but the Dow Theory for the twenty-first century since then.

The fourth buy signal is when the markets reach the definition of a bull market. When a +19 percent move up from the lows as measured by the Dow Jones Industrial Average (DJIA) *and* the Standard & Poor's 500 Index (S&P 500) has occurred, it has been followed 95 percent of the time by a further upmove to +29 percent and 50 percent of the time by a move to +80 percent.

The three types of sell signals are the Dow Theory, the Schannep Timing Indicator, and the definition of a bear market having been met. When the market has dropped –16 percent, the definition of a bear market, it has then gone on 83 percent of the time to drop to –21 percent and nearly 46 percent of the time (11 of 24 times) has gone to at least –35 percent. Since *all* bull and bear markets meeting the definition have progressed further and been joined belatedly by the Dow Theory or the Schannep Timing Indicator, if not already on board, this Indicator should be used to complete to 100 percent *in* or *out* of the market.

On the first buy or sell signal, go to 50 percent invested. When *any* of the specified signals follow, you should move from 50 to 100 percent in or out of the market. The one exception would be a second capitulation, at which time only an additional 25 percent is added. As exceptional as this buy indicator has been, we do not want to base this composite indicator's signals on just one underlying type of signal. Therefore, it would take a signal of the second, third, or fourth type to complete the move to 100 percent in or out of the market.

I hope this is clear. If not, I suggest you look through the complete record in Appendix D with an eye to following specific actions taken during any of the various signals. You'll note that I have not included a graphic representation of the Composite Indicator because it is often partially, if not totally, "in" or "out" of the market, as opposed to the Dow Theory, which is usually all the way in or all the way out of the market. The dates and price levels, as well as the dollar results, for the complete 50+ year record are shown in Appendix D.

Table 13.1 Composite Indicator Buy Signals and the S&P 500 Gains Thereafter

Completion BUY Date	Average Level	3 Months Level	3 Months Gain	6 Months Level	6 Months Gain	9 Months Level	9 Months Gain	1 Year Level	1 Year Gain	To SELL Signal SELL Date	To SELL Signal Ave. Level	To SELL Signal Gain
1/25/1954	25.81	27.78	7.6%	30.31	17.4%	31.96	23.8%	35.51	37.6%	10/1/1956	44.70	73.2%
5/5/1958	43.79	47.75	9.0%	52.03	18.8%	54.81	25.2%	57.75	31.9%	3/3/1960	54.78	25.1%
10/10/1961	62.84	68.96	9.7%	68.56	9.1%	65.31	3.9%			5/10/1962	65.31	3.9%
11/9/1962	55.73	66.17	18.7%	70.35	26.2%	70.48	26.5%	73.36	31.6%	5/5/1966	87.84	57.6%
1/11/1967	83.47	88.88	6.5%	92.48	10.8%	96.37	15.5%	95.52	14.4%	1/22/1968	98.20	17.6%
10/1/1968	102.86	103.86	1.0%	98.32	-4.4%					3/1/1969	98.32	-4.4%
10/27/1969*	97.94	88.17	-5.0%							1/26/1970	88.17	-5.0%
8/24/1970	72.94	84.78	16.2%	96.73	32.6%	100.13	37.3%	98.74	35.4%	3/23/1973	112.53	52.0%
10/22/1973*	109.16	98.66	-4.8%							11/20/1973	98.66	-9.6%
11/4/1974	69.34	77.61	11.9%	89.22	28.7%	87.15	25.7%	88.51	27.6%	10/31/1977	92.34	33.2%
6/6/1978	97.39	105.38	8.2%	97.68	0.3%					10/26/1978	97.68	0.3%
6/11/1980	111.16	125.66	13.0%	127.36	14.6%	129.95	16.9%	133.75	20.3%	8/31/1981	125.72	13.1%
9/3/1982	119.40	138.69	16.2%	153.48	28.5%	164.42	37.7%	165.00	38.2%	2/22/1984	164.10	37.4%
1/21/1985	171.53	181.11	5.6%	195.13	13.8%	186.96	9.0%	205.79	20.0%	10/16/1987	290.39	69.3%
1/7/1988	233.99	266.16	13.7%	271.78	16.2%	278.07	18.8%	280.67	19.9%	8/27/1998	1072.12	358.2%
11/2/1998	1034.44	1261.99	22.0%	1335.18	29.1%	1328.05	28.4%	1252.21	21.1%	9/23/1999	1252.21	21.1%
12/3/1999*	1433.30	1409.17	-0.9%	1477.26	1.5%	1520.77	3.0%	1315.23	-4.1%	3/16/2001	1150.53	-9.9%
11/6/2001	1031.51	1083.51	5.0%	1052.67	2.1%	997.33	-3.3%			7/3/2002	997.33	-3.3%
8/14/2002	870.33	904.27	6.9%	834.89	0.7%	939.28	10.2%	990.51	15.6%	1/15/2008	1403.37	+61.27
Average:			**8.9%**		**15.4%**		**19.9%**		**25.8%**			**20.8%**
Average Annual Gain Buy to Sell including dividends:												

Completion Dates reflect when the Buy percentage gets to 100%. The level is the average of the entered levels.

*These were only entered to the 50% level so results are adjusted appropriately.

If partial or full Sells come in before the Year is complete the levels reflect the appropriate exit levels and date.

In the case of the 8/14/02 Buy the sells and buybacks are accounted for in the appropriate time frame.

Table 13.2   Composite Indicator Sell Signals and the Further Dow Jones Industrial Loss to the Final Bear Market Lows (data since January 19, 1954)

Sell Date:	Average Level	Low Date	Level	Further Loss	Months to Low
10/1/1956	489.97	10/22/1957	419.79	14.3%	12.7
3/3/1960	628.16	10/25/1960	566.05*	9.9%	7.7
5/10/1962	662.96	6/26/1962	535.76	19.2%	1.5
5/5/1966	915.86	10/7/1966	744.32	18.7%	5.0
1/22/1968	879.95	3/21/1968	825.13*	6.2%	2.0
3/7/1969	905.49	5/26/1970	631.16	30.3%	14.6
7/28/1971**	872.01	11/23/1971	797.97	8.5%	3.8
3/23/1973	941.00	8/22/1973	851.90*	9.5%	5.0
10/31/1977	810.34	2/28/1978	742.12	8.4%	4.0
10/26/1978	833.76	4/21/1980	759.13	9.0%	5.8
8/31/1981	920.33	8/12/1982	776.92	15.6%	11.4
2/22/1984	1183.05	7/24/1984	1086.57*	8.2%	5.1
10/16/1987	2300.91	10/19/1987	1738.74	24.4%	0.1
10/13/1989**	2569.26	1/30/1990	2543.24*	1.0%	3.6
8/3/1990**	2809.65	10/11/1990	2365.10	15.8%	2.3
6/20/1994**	3741.90	6/30/1994	3624.96*	3.1%	0.3
8/27/1998	8326.26	8/31/1998	7539.07	9.5%	0.1
9/23/1999	10621.56	10/15/1999	10019.71*	5.7%	0.7
7/3/2002	9382.38	7/23/2002	7702.34*	17.9%	3.2
9/17/2002**	8207.55	10/9/2002	7286.27	11.2%	0.7
1/24/2003**	8131.01	3/11/2003	7524.06*	7.5%	1.6
8/5/2004***	9981.02	10/25/2004	9749.99*	2.3%	2.6
7/12/2006**	11013.18	9/14/2006	10739.35*	2.5%	2.1
1/15/2008	12765.02				
	Average further decline:			**11.2%**	**4.2**

*When no "official" Bear market follows, this is the low for this move.
**This was a 50% Sell.
***This was a 75% Sell.
12 Signals were followed by "official" Bear markets; 11 were not.
9 completed signals were followed by "official" Bear markets; 6 were not.

My backtesting studies have shown that this Composite Indicator would have captured some 84 percent of bull market total points over the last 50+ years. It would have been invested in all or part of the 29 best *months* since 1954 and was invested in the market fully 86 percent of the time during those months. During the 25 best *years*, it was in a buy mode some 93 percent of the time. In the case of bear markets, the Composite Indicator was in a sell mode, which would have avoided just over 50 percent of the losses that come with bear markets.

In Table 13.1 you can see the short-term results following Composite buy signals over the next 3 months, 6 months, 9 months, and a year. In Chapter 14, you will see that this record is the best of all the various individual indicators covered in this book, except for capitulation during the first year following a signal.

Table 13.2 shows the further downside moves after a Composite sell signal, with the average being a further loss of −11.2 percent over an average of 4.2 months.

The record of the Composite Indicator is not perfect, of course, but it comes as close as possible to being the ideal market indicator over the long term. This combination of Dow Theory, the Schannep Timing Indicator, capitulation, and the definitions of bull and bear markets has truly gained synergy.

CHAPTER

14

Practical Uses

PUTTING IT ALL TOGETHER

After reading 13 chapters about the components and various ways to invest successfully in the stock market, it is time to put it all together. In this chapter, we discuss "what" to do after the "when" has been determined by our indicators. We discuss how much to invest and remind you how to review the status of the stock market, the economy, and the indicators. Finally, you will see the results of the indicators covered in this book all lined up in one place, side by side. This should prepare you to improve your investment results, which is, after all, the purpose of this book.

After When, Then What?

This book answers the difficult question of when to buy and when to sell, with results that are both verified and superior to a buy-and-hold strategy. Not many other books, newsletters, or web sites can make that claim and back it up. Three specific examples of buy signals generated from the Indicators in this book were on December 7, 1987, when I proclaimed in my Market Letter: "They say no one rings a bell at market lows . . . but listen closely: I just did!" That was *the* day the market turned up from the lows for the Standard & Poor's (S&P) 500 Index and started a 72 percent gain over the next two and three-quarters years. On the evening of September 20, 2001, I sent out an e-mail entitled "Today we got TOTAL capitulation" that said to "BUY if you have been following our Dow Theory Sell signal over the last two years and are out of the market, or if you are in the market but currently underinvested . . . this is the stuff of market lows." The next morning was *the* low of the market on the way to a 29 percent gain over the next six months. The next e-mail, "ONLY TWICE BEFORE IN 50 YEARS, AND NOW TODAY," went out the afternoon of October 9, 2002, *the* low of the twenty-first century, after which the market gained 94+ percent over the next five years. But after knowing "when," the next logical question is now: "What do I do?"

Because market timing as espoused in this book is concerned with the major United States markets, the most appropriate investment vehicles are American Stock Exchange Traded Funds (ETFs) that track the S&P 500 (Spiders), the Dow Jones Industrial Average (Diamonds), or the New York Stock Exchange Composite Index (NYC iShares). They trade like stocks, and the dividends are distributed quarterly, equivalent to the dividends paid by the underlying stocks in the unit investment trust, less annual fees of about 0.18 percent. Spiders (SPY) track the Standard & Poor's 500 Index. Diamonds (DIA) are similar and are often called "index shares on the Dow." Similarly the iShares New York Stock Exchange Composite (NYC) is an index fund tracking the NYSE Composite Index.

From time to time "new" stocks are substituted in the various indices for those that are deemed no longer representative. Thus the performances of the ETFs are often enhanced by these adjustments. In the late 1990s, the advantage was greater for the S&P because of more computer, Internet, and technology-related stocks held among its 500 stock portfolio than are included in the Dow Jones 30 stocks. That is not to say that the Dow Jones cannot and will not outperform the S&P over any period; in fact, that is exactly what happened in 1999 when the Dow gained 25.2 percent while the S&P gained 19.5 percent, almost the opposite of 1998, when the S&P gained 26.7 percent and the Dow gained 16.1 percent. In the years 2000 through 2002, both lost ground with the Dow losing less than the S&P.

All major indices have risen since 2002, but the Dow Jones Industrial Average lagged behind the S&P 500 Index for a time after August 2003. The Dow rose only 17.4 percent while the S&P rose 27.9 percent. How does that happen? Well, for one thing, the Dow added three stocks in April 2004 that all fell in price and removed three stocks of which two rose. When there are only 30 stocks in the average, just a few can make a big difference. In 2005, General Motors fell 50 percent and had a greater impact on the Dow Jones than it did on the S&P 500. Further, there was only one oil stock in the Dow. The S&P has more than a dozen, and that industry was performing very well. It is also true that the S&P 500 dropped more from 2000 to 2002 so its stronger rebound was appropriate.

These differing results are the very reason I suggest investing in the three indices, in order to obtain an average that is midway between them. Since there is no way of knowing a year ahead of time which index will perform best in that year, a combination of Spiders, Diamonds, and the NYSE iShares will assure full participation in the market's move.

How much you invest is an individual decision. When I recommend "fully invested," that usually means near-totally invested *with those funds that are earmarked for investment.* Perhaps you always keep 5 or 10 percent in cash "just in case," and that's fine. An aggressive pension fund would probably only go to 80 percent maximum, with 5 to 10 percent in cash and 10 to 15 percent in bonds. Incidentally, the standard blend for asset allocation is always at 55 percent stocks, 35 percent bonds, and 10 percent cash. That allocation almost always beats the performance of the recommended blends of the major brokerage firms.

When there is a sell signal, if you are a very aggressive investor you would sell most of what you hold with the possible exception of low-cost core holdings. An institution would seldom sell as much as 50 percent of its portfolio, and that is probably true for most serious long-term investors as well. The cash portion should be held in money market funds, short-term certificates of deposit, Treasury notes, and the like.

I do not recommend selling short in my newsletter or in this book because that is not appropriate for many, if not most, readers. Selling short "against the box" is appropriate for many investors with low-cost core holdings as a hedge against a falling market. In that case, you keep your original stock position but sell some offsetting shares short; therefore, what you "lose" from the market's highs on your underlying stock you will gain on your short sales, it is hoped. Then, when it is time to buy, you simply cover the short position and continue on with your holding of your original stock without any tax consequence. The short gain is of course taxed at short-term rates. For tax advice, you should talk to your tax advisor.

And Now If You're Ready to Put It All Together, What . . . ?

In order to determine where we are at any given time in the stock market—whether it's too late to buy, too early to sell, or what— I consider three different but equal elements:

1. **The status of the stock market.** Is it in a bull or a bear market? The definitions in this book should make that clear enough, and the chances of its status continuing can be guesstimated from the historical record and from the bell curves. The quartiles as to both price change and longevity can be used as a *guide*. Other factors can be considered, such as the time since the start of the bull or bear market. For instance, the first year of bull markets is almost always the strongest and the fourth and fifth years also tend to be very favorable *for those bull markets that last that long*. The percentage of bull markets completing their first year is very high: 84 percent, and this is certainly the time you would want to be invested. The number of bull markets that have lasted three years and then go on to complete the fourth year is an even higher 87.5 percent, but the longer a bull market lasts the closer it is, by definition, to ending, so the later years carry more risk. The time of year may be worth some consideration in fine-tuning. January is usually a good time to start, as is after both January and February if both were up. July through October may not be as good, unless perhaps it is a presidential pre-election or election year.

2. **The status of the economy.** Is it in an expansion or a recession? This should be obvious from the news of the day (not from the National Bureau of Economic Research), but if not, look to Chapter 11 for clues of expansions ending. The Indicators included in "Three Tops and a Tumble" point to recessions starting. Capacity utilization and non-farm payrolls turning up are excellent indicators for determining the end of recessions and start of expansions.

3. **The status of the market timing indicators.** Are they in buy or sell modes? That status should give you the confidence to take an investment stance. In a bull market, keep track of where the stick in the sand is. Look for pullbacks that then turn to a bounce that could rise 3 percent without making

new highs. Don't anticipate changes in direction but be vigilant; they can happen at any time. If the market's momentum and the monetary status are both favorable, then the market should continue in an uptrend. In a bear market, look for capitulation to occur as a turning point. This book highlights eight capitulation indicators for identifying market bottoms, but as you know, my Capitulation Indicator has been better more times than any of the others. Table 14.1 shows the results of the indicators covered in this book following their buy and sell signals excluding dividends.

You would expect that the capitulation indicator, which is almost *always the first* signal to be given, would have the best record from its buy signal during the first year. It *is* usually the first out of the chute and has an excellent first 3-, 6-, 9-, and 12-month record. Surprisingly, the Composite Indicator catches up with it at the 1-year mark, partly because the time frame is different. You'll recall that the time after its signal is measured from when the *last* component takes it to 100 percent invested. In other words, the first year does not start and end at the same time for each indicator. The number of samples varies for each indicator over the last 50+ years that each was tracked. Capitulation has the fewest and, of course, has no sell signal associated with it. The "Official" bull/bear data is used from January 1, 1946; the Dow Theory for the twenty-first century started November 29, 1957; all others began December 31, 1953. The number of samples range from 11 for capitulation to over 20 for the Dow Theory indicators.

Table 14.1 Wrap-Up of the Results

Indicator: BUYS	3 Months % Gain	6 Months % Gain	9 Months % Gain	1 Year % Gain	Average Annual Gain Buy to Sell
"Official" Bull market	3.6	9.1	10.0	16.7	12.8*
Schannep Timing Indicator	7.8	14.9	18.0	22.2	17.0
Original Dow Theory	5.1	11.6	14.3	19.5	18.7
21st-century Dow Theory	4.7	10.2	16.8	19.5	20.5
Composite Indicator	8.9	15.4	19.9	25.8	20.8
Capitulation only	11.0	18.5	24.7	25.4	n/a†

*Sell is to "official" bear status attained.

†No sell is associated with this indicator.

Table 14.2   Further Market Decline after Sell Signals

Indicator: SELLS	Further Decline to Market Lows	Time to Market Lows
Composite Indicator	−11.2%	4.2 months
"Official" Bear market	−12.0%	6.1
Schannep Timing Indicator	−12.5%	4.9
Original Dow Theory	−12.8%	5.6
21st-century Dow Theory	−14.6%	5.5

The best record for the annual average gain *from buy to sell* is important as that measures the results during the time you are *in* the market. The time *out* of the market is invested in money market funds or the like, while the asset value is being maintained. I wouldn't dwell too much on the variations in quarterly results as all are excellent, even if you wait for the bull market to become official.

For sell signals, the indicator followed by the most market decline is the Dow Theory for the twenty-first century, as shown in Table 14.2. The results for the Composite Indicator are somewhat distorted by partial sells, which the other indicators do not usually have. Whichever signal you rely on, a significant further decline would seem to be likely.

A Final Thought

As I set out in the Introduction, I sincerely hope this book has provided you with a better understanding of the ingredients that make up the world of finance, specifically the American stock market, and that that understanding leads you to great investment success. Whether you invest on your own with some of the ideas you learned in this book or rely on a professional for help is a matter of individual circumstance and preference. I wish you good fortune in whatever you do.

"Official" Complete and Detailed Record of the Original Dow Theory

There really is no "official" record of the original Dow Theory, or at least none anointed by Charles Dow himself. I do not presume that all Dow Theorists will agree with each and every signal in Table A.1, but from what I have been able to gather from multiple respectable sources plus my own interpretation, I do feel this is as close as one is going to get to an official record. The details (after 1919) will help you understand how the signals were constructed.

Table A.1　Dow Theory Buy and Sell Signals over the Years

Dow Theory	Date	Industrial Average	% Change	Status	Date	Transport Average	% Change
BUY	7/12/1897	44.61					
SELL	12/16/99	63.84					
	9/24/1900	52.96		Bear market low			
BUY	10/20/00	59.44					
	6/17/01	78.26		Bull market high			
SELL	6/1/03	59.59					
	11/9/03	42.15		Bear market low			
BUY	7/12/04	51.37					
	1/19/06	103.00		Bull market high			
SELL	4/26/06	92.44					
	11/15/07	53.00		Bear market low			
BUY	4/24/08	70.01					
	11/19/09	100.53		Bull market high			
SELL	5/3/10	84.72					
BUY	10/10/10	81.91					
	9/25/11	72.94		Bear market low			
	9/30/12	94.15		Bull market high			
SELL	1/14/13	84.96					
	12/24/14	53.17*		Bear market low			
BUY	4/9/15	65.02					
	11/21/16	110.15		Bull market high			
SELL	8/28/17	86.12					
	12/19/17	65.95		Bear market low			
BUY	5/13/18	82.16					
	11/3/19	119.62		Bull market high	5/26	91.13	
	12/22	103.55	13.4	Pullback	12/12	73.63	19.2
	1/3/20	109.88	6.1	Bounce	1/3	76.48	3.9
	1/14	102.00		Breakdown	2/3	73.56	

Dow Theory	Date	Industrial Average	% Change	Status	Date	Transport Average	% Change
SELL	2/3/20	99.96				73.56	
(S-1)	8/24/21	63.90		*Bear market low*	6/20/21	65.52	
	12/15	81.50	27.5	Bounce	11/29	76.66	17.0
	1/10/22	78.59	3.6	Pullback	12/23	73.30	4.4
	1/17	81.90		Breakup	2/6	76.70	
BUY	2/6/22	83.70				76.70	
(B-1)	10/14	103.43		Market highs	9/11	93.99	
	11/27	92.03	11.0	Pullback	11/27	82.17	12.6
	3/20/23	105.38	14.5	*Bull high/* Bounce	3/3	90.63	10.3
	5/21	92.77	12.0	Pullback	5/7	80.37	
	5/29	97.66	5.3	Bounce			
SELL	6/20/23	90.81		Breakdown		80.60	
(S-2)	7/31	86.91		Market lows	8/4	76.78	
	8/29	93.70	7.8	Bounce	10/6	80.81	5.2
	10/27	85.76	8.5	*Bear low/* Pullback	10/26	77.65	3.9
BUY	12/7/23	93.80		Breakup	11/13	81.20	
(B-2)	9/3/29	381.17		*Bull market high*	9/3	189.11	
	10/4	325.17	14.7	Pullback	10/4	168.26	11.0
	10/10	352.86	8.5	Bounce	10/11	178.53	6.1
	10/19	323.87		Breakdown	10/23	167.28	
SELL	10/23/29	305.85					
(S-1)	7/8/32	41.22		*Bear market low*	7/8	13.23	
	9/7	79.93	93.9	Bounce	9/3	39.27	196.8
	2/27	50.16	37.2	Pullback	2/25	23.43	40.3
BUY	5/24/33	84.29		Breakup	5/24	40.28	
(B-1)	3/10/37	194.40		*Bull market high*	3/17	64.46	
	6/14	165.51	14.9	Pullback	6/28	50.17	22.2
	8/14	190.02	14.8	Bounce	7/24	55.05	9.7
SELL	9/7/37	164.39		Breakdown	8/27	49.40	
(S-1)	3/31/38	98.95		*Bear market low*	3/31	19.00	
	4/16	121.00	22.3	Bounce	5/9	23.50	23.7
	5/31	107.74	11.0	Pullback	6/17	19.68	16.3
	6/21	121.34		Breakup	6/23	24.60	

(continued)

Table A.1   (*continued*)

Dow Theory	Date	Industrial Average	% Change	Status	Date	Transport Average	% Change
BUY	6/23/38	127.40					
(B-1)	11/12	158.41		*Bull market high*	1/4/39	34.33	
	1/26/39	136.42	13.9	Pullback	1/26	27.93	18.6
	3/10	152.28	11.6	Bounce	3/8	33.66	20.5
SELL	3/31/39	131.84		Breakdown	3/31	26.38	
(S-1)	4/8	121.44		Market lows	4/8	24.14	
	6/10	140.14	15.4	Bounce	5/31	28.45	17.9
	6/29	130.05	7.2	Pullback	6/30	25.85	9.1
BUY	7/17/39	142.58		Breakup	7/17	29.14	
(B-1)	9/12	155.92		Market highs	9/27	35.90	
	1/15/40	144.65	7.2	Pullback	3/16	29.78	17.0
	4/8	151.29	4.6	Bounce	4/6	32.08	7.7
SELL	5/13/40	137.63		Breakdown	5/13	27.83	
(S-1)	4/28/42	92.92		*Bear market low*	5/21/40	22.14	
	11/9	117.30	26.2	Bounce	11/2	29.28	32.2
	11/24	114.10	2.7	Pullback	12/14	26.03	11.1
	12/17	118.68		Breakup	2/1/43	29.55	
BUY	2/1/43	125.86					
(B-2)	5/29/46	212.50		*Bull market high*	6/13/46	69.31	
	7/22	195.22	8.1	Pullback	7/23	60.41	12.8
	8/13	204.52	4.8	Bounce	8/2	63.63	5.3
SELL	8/27/46	191.04		Breakdown	8/27	58.04	
(S-1)	5/17/47	163.21		Market lows	5/19/47	41.16	
	7/24	186.85	14.5	Bounce	1/2/48	53.85	30.8
	3/16/48	165.39	11.5	Pullback	2/10	48.13	10.6
BUY	5/14/48	188.60		Breakup	4/3	53.93	
(B-1)	6/15	193.16		Market highs	7/14	64.95	
	9/27	175.99	8.9	Pullback	9/27	57.45	11.5
	10/23	190.19	8.1	Bounce	10/23	62.24	8.3
SELL	11/9/48	173.94		Breakdown	11/5	56.22	
(S-1)	6/13/49	161.60		*Bear market low*	6/13	41.03	
	6/12/50	228.38	41.3	Bounce	5/20	56.96	38.8
	7/13	197.46	13.5	Pullback	6/29	51.24	10.0
BUY	10/2/50	228.94		Breakup	7/19	57.10	
(B-1)	1/5/53	293.79		Market highs	12/22/52	112.53	

Dow Theory	Date	Industrial Average	% Change	Status	Date	Transport Average	% Change
	2/18	281.14	4.3	Pullback	2/10	106.90	5.0
	3/17	290.64	3.4	Bounce	3/17	112.03	4.8
	3/31	279.87		Breakdown	4/2	106.11	
SELL	4/2/53	280.03					
(S-1)	9/14	255.49		Market lows	9/14	90.56	
	12/18	283.54	11.0	Bounce	12/1	98.91	9.2
	12/29	278.30	1.8	Pullback	12/29	93.58	5.4
	1/6/54	283.96		Breakup	1/19/54	99.43	
BUY	1/19/54	288.27					
(B-5)	4/6/56	521.05		Bull market high	5/9	181.23	
	5/28	468.81	10.0	Pullback	5/28	161.60	10.8
	8/2	520.95	11.1	Bounce	7/25	171.37	6.0
SELL	10/1/56	468.70		Breakdown	8/22	161.28	
(S-1)	10/22/57	419.79		Bear market low	12/24	95.67	
	2/4/58	458.65	9.3	Bounce	2/4	111.16	16.2
	2/25	436.89	4.7	Pullback	4/7	100.67	9.4
BUY	5/2/58	459.56		Breakup	4/21	111.60	
(B-1)	8/3/59	678.10		Market highs	7/7	173.56	
	9/22	616.45	9.1	Pullback	11/17	146.65	15.5
	1/5/60	685.47	11.2	New high/ Bounce	1/5	160.43	9.4
	2/16	611.33		Breakdown	3/3	142.98	
SELL	3/3/60	612.05					
(S-2)	10/25	566.05		Market lows	9/29	123.37	
	4/17/61	696.72	23.1	Bounce	3/22	150.81	22.2
	4/24	672.66	3.5	Pullback	4/25	140.04	7.1
	5/19	705.96		Bounce/lower	5/17	148.02	
	7/18	679.30		Pullback/ lower	7/19	133.49	
	7/27	702.80					
BUY	10/10/61	706.67		Breakup	10/10	150.91	
(B-3)	12/13/61	734.91		Bull market high	10/11	152.92	
	1/29/62	689.92	6.1	Pullback	12/20	140.66	8.0
	3/15	723.54	4.9	Bounce	2/2	149.83	6.5
	4/12	685.67		Breakdown	4/26	140.28	

(continued)

Table A.1   (continued)

Dow Theory	Date	Industrial Average	% Change	Status	Date	Transport Average	% Change
SELL	4/26/62	678.68					
(S-1)	6/26	535.76		Bear market low	6/25	115.89	
	8/23	616.00	15.0	Bounce	7/16	125.49	8.3
	10/23	558.06	9.4	Pullback	10/1	114.86	8.5
BUY	11/9/62	616.13		Breakup	11/9	126.05	
(B-1)	2/9/66	995.15		Bull market high	2/15	271.72	
	3/15	911.08	8.4	Pullback	3/15	243.60	10.3
	4/21	954.73	4.8	Bounce	4/20	265.97	9.2
SELL	5/5/66	899.77		Breakdown	5/5	240.96	
(S-1)	10/7	744.32		Bear market low	10/7	184.34	
	11/16	820.87	10.3	Bounce	11/16	208.79	13.3
	12/2	789.47	3.8	Pullback	11/22	199.54	4.4
	12/12	820.54		Lower/ Bounce	12/22	209.07	
	12/30	785.69		Lower/ Pullback	12/30	202.97	
BUY	1/11/67	822.49		Breakup	1/6	209.19	
(B-3)	8/9	926.72		Market highs	8/4	274.49	
	8/30	893.72	3.6	Pullback	8/22	256.06	6.7
	9/25	943.08	5.5	New high/ Bounce	9/18	265.11	3.5
SELL	10/24/67	888.18		Breakdown	10/10	254.59	
(S-2)	3/21/68	825.13		Market lows	3/5	214.58	
	7/15	923.72	11.9	Bounce	7/8	269.61	25.6
	8/9	869.65	5.9	Pullback	8/9	245.76	8.8
	9/9	924.98		Breakup	10/1	270.24	
BUY	10/1/68	942.32					
(B-1)	12/3	985.21		Bull market high	12/1	279.48	
	1/8/69	921.25	6.5	Pullback	1/13	260.04	7.0
	2/13	952.70	3.4	Bounce/New high	2/7	279.88	7.6
	2/20	916.65		Breakdown	2/25	257.07	
SELL	2/25/69	899.80					
(S-2)	7/29	801.96		Market lows	7/30	193.19	
	9/2	837.78	4.5	Bounce	8/22	202.02	4.6

Dow Theory	Date	Industrial Average	% Change	Status	Date	Transport Average	% Change
	9/8	811.84	3.1	Pullback	10/9	194.72	3.6
	10/16	838.77		Breakup	10/27	202.37	
BUY	10/27/69	860.28					
(B-1)	11/10	863.05		Market highs	10/28	202.45	
	12/17	769.93	10.8	Pullback	12/16	169.43	16.3
	1/5/70	811.31	5.4	Bounce	1/5	183.31	8.2
SELL	1/26/70	768.88		Breakdown	1/26	168.98	
(S-1)	5/26	631.16		*Bear market low*	5/26	131.53	
	6/19	720.43	14.1	Bounce	6/3	146.98	11.7
	7/7	669.36	7.1	Pullback/ *New low*	7/7	116.69	20.6
	7/16	723.44		Breakup	9/28	148.21	
BUY	9/28/70	758.97					
(B-2)	4/28/71	950.82		Market highs	4/28	232.79	
	6/28	873.10	8.2	Pullback	6/28	208.89	10.3
	7/12	903.40	3.5	Bounce	7/12	220.21	5.4
SELL	7/28/71	872.01		Breakdown	7/28	208.06	
(S-1)	8/10	839.59		Market lows	8/4	203.61	
	9/8	920.93	9.7	Bounce	9/7	248.33	22.0
	11/23	797.97	13.4	New low/ Pullback	11/23	208.43	16.1
BUY	2/10/72	921.28		Breakup	1/12	249.08	
(B-2)	1/11/73	1051.7		*Bull market high*	12/11/72	240.41	
	2/27	947.72	9.9	Pullback	3/5	191.58	20.3
	3/7	979.98	3.4	Bounce	3/7	198.35	3.5
SELL	3/23/73	922.71		Breakdown	3/23	189.22	
(S-1)	10/4/74	584.56		Market lows	10/3	125.93	
	10/14	673.50	15.2	Bounce	10/22	152.74	21.3
	10/28	633.84	5.9	Pullback	10/28	145.78	4.6
BUY	11/5/74	674.75		Breakup	11/1	153.55	
(B-1)	12/6	577.60		*Bear low/* Pullback	12/16	138.31	
	9/21/76	1014.79		*Bull market high*	7/14	231.27	
	10/12	932.35	8.1	Pullback	10/12	203.85	11.9
	12/31	1004.65	7.8	Bounce/New high	1/03/77	237.52	16.5

(continued)

Table A.1   (continued)

Dow Theory	Date	Industrial Average	% Change	Status	Date	Transport Average	% Change
	5/31/77	898.66		New low/ Pullback	2/25	221.81	
	6/24	929.70		Bounce/New high	5/18	246.64	
	7/27	888.43		Breakdown	8/9	220.88	
SELL	10/24/77	802.32		Break 1st pullback	10/24	201.74	
(S-3)	2/28/78	742.72		*Bear market low*	3/9	199.31	
	5/17	858.37	15.6	Bounce	5/22	231.30	16.1
	5/26	831.69	3.1	Pullback	5/26	223.70	3.3
	6/5	863.83		Breakup	6/6	231.35	
BUY	6/6/78	866.51					
(B-1)	9/11	907.74		*Bull market high*	9/8	261.49	
	9/20	857.16	5.6	Pullback	9/22	241.58	7.6
	10/11	901.42	5.2	Bounce	10/12	250.15	3.5
SELL	10/19/78	846.41		Breakdown	10/17	237.44	
(S-1)	3/27/80	759.98		Market lows	3/27	233.69	
	4/11	791.55	4.2	Bounce	4/10	253.46	8.5
	4/21/80	759.13	4.1	*Bear low/ Pullback*	4/21	235.20	7.2
	4/24	797.10		Breakup	5/13	253.83	
BUY	5/13/80	816.89					
(B-1)	4/27/81	1024.05		*Bull market high*	4/16	447.38	
	5/11	963.44	5.9	Pullback	5/11	410.28	8.3
	6/15	1011.99	5.0	Bounce	6/1	430.92	5.0
SELL	7/2/81	959.19		Breakdown	7/2	409.60	
(S-1)	8/12/82	776.92		*Bear market low*	8/12	292.12	
	9/21	934.79	20.3	Bounce	9/14	375.45	28.5
	9/30	896.25	4.1	Pullback	9/30	360.46	4.0
	10/6	944.26		Breakup	10/7		
BUY	10/7/82	965.97					
(B-1)	11/29/83	1287.20		Market highs	11/22	612.57	
	12/15	1236.79	3.9	Pullback	12/22	587.07	4.2
	1/6/84	1286.64	4.0	Bounce/New high	1/9	612.63	4.4

Dow Theory	Date	Industrial Average	% Change	Status	Date	Transport Average	% Change
SELL	1/25/84	1231.89		Breakdown	1/24	585.29	
(S-2)	7/24	1086.57		Market lows	7/25	444.03	
	9/17	1237.52	13.9	Bounce	9/14	526.52	18.6
	12/7	1163.21	6.0	Pullback	10/9	508.48	3.4
BUY	1/21/85	1261.37		Breakup	10/18	542.53	
(B-1)	8/25/87	2722.42		*Bull market high*	8/14	1101.16	
	9/21	2492.82	8.4	Pullback	9/21	1005.80	8.7
	10/2	2640.99	5.9	Bounce	10/2	1064.41	5.8
	10/14	2412.70		Breakdown	10/15	980.24	
SELL	10/15/87	2355.09					
(S-1)	10/19	1738.74		*Bear market low*	10/20	740.25	
	10/21	2027.85	16.6	Bounce	10/21	787.01	6.3
	10/26	1793.93	11.5	Pullback/New low	10/26	674.92	14.2
	11/2	2014.09		Lower bounce	11/2	784.38	
	12/4	1766.74		Lower pullback/ *New low*	12/4	661.00	
	1/5/88	2031.50		Breakup	1/7	789.43	
BUY	1/7/88	2051.89					
(B-4)	9/1/89	2752.09		Market highs	9/5	1532.01	
	9/25	2659.19	3.4	Pullback	9/26	1424.96	7.0
	10/9	2791.41	5.0	New high/ Bounce	10/9	1518.49	6.6
SELL	10/13/89	2569.26		Breakdown	10/13	1406.29	
(S-2)	1/30	2543.24		Market lows	1/30	1031.83	
	4/17	2765.77	8.7	Bounce	3/27	1192.57	15.6
	4/27	2645.05	4.4	Pullback	4/27	1128.20	5.4
	5/11	2801.58		Breakup	6/4	1207.85	
BUY	6/4/90	2935.19					
(B-1)	6/15	2935.89		Market highs	6/6	1212.77	
	6/26	2842.33	3.2	Pullback	7/5	1131.02	6.7
	7/16	2999.75	5.5	*Bull high/* Bounce	7/16	1189.60	5.2
SELL	8/3/90	2809.65		Breakdown	7/30	1125.00	
(S-2)	10/11	2365.10		*Bear market low*	10/17	821.93	

(continued)

Table A.1   (*continued*)

Dow Theory	Date	Industrial Average	% Change	Status	Date	Transport Average	% Change
	10/19	2520.79	6.6	Bounce	10/22	883.69	7.5
	10/29	2430.20	3.6	Pullback	10/31	822.30	6.9
	11/12	2540.35		Breakup	12/5	903.67	
BUY	12/5/90	2610.40					
(B-1)	5/13/98	9211.84		Market highs	4/16	3686.02	
	6/15	8627.93	6.3	Pullback	6/2	3259.30	11.6
	7/17	9337.97	8.2	*Bull high/* Bounce	7/14	3618.73	11.0
SELL	8/4/98	8487.31		Breakdown	7/29	3244.93	
(S-2)	8/31	7539.07		*Bear market low*	9/4	2616.75	
	9/23	8154.41	8.1	Bounce	9/23	2904.10	11.0
	10/1	7632.53	6.4	Pullback/ *Newer low*	10/8	2345.00	19.3
	10/15	8299.36		Breakup	11/2	2954.83	
BUY	11/2/98	8706.50					
(B-1)	5/13/99	11107.19		Market highs	5/12/99	3783.50	
	5/27	10466.93	5.8	Pullback	6/25	3316.11	12.4
	7/16	11209.84	7.1	Market high/ Bounce	7/2	3515.99	6.0
	8/2	10645.96		Pullback/New low	8/11	3130.53	
	8/25	11326.04		Market high/ Bounce	8/25	3309.25	
SELL	9/23/99	10318.59		Break 1st pullback	9/23	2895.98	
(S-3)	1/14/2000	11722.98		*Bull market high*			
	9/21/01	8235.81		*Bear market low*	9/20	2033.86	
	10/26	9545.17	15.9	Bounce	10/11	2314.80	13.8
	10/31	9075.14	4.9	Pullback	10/19	2174.28	6.1
	11/6	9591.12		Breakup	11/8	2320.98	
BUY	11/8/01	9587.52					
(B-1)	3/19/02	10635.25		*Bull market high*	3/4	3049.96	
	5/6	9808.04	7.8	Pullback	5/10	2643.10	13.5
	5/18	10353.08	5.5	Bounce	5/17	2798.36	5.8
	6/3	9709.79		Breakdown	6/25	2627.92	

Dow Theory	Date	Industrial Average	% Change	Status	Date	Transport Average	% Change
SELL	6/25/02	9126.80					
(S-1)	10/9	7286.27		Bear market low	10/9	2013.02	
	11/27	8931.68	22.6	Bounce	11/6	2413.71	19.9
	3/11/03	7524.06	15.8	Pullback/ Newer low	3/11	1942.19	19.5
BUY	6/4/03	9038.98		Breakup	5/2	2460.80	
(B-2)	7/19	14000.41		Market highs	7/19	5446.49	
	8/16	12845.78	8.2	Pullback	8/16	4671.88	14.2
	10/9	14164.53	10.3	Newer high/ Bounce	10/5	4997.17	7.0
SELL (S-2)	11/21/07	12799.04		Breakdown	11/7	4663.35	

*Changed basis was 71.00.

Author's note: The buy signal in November 1998 is different from the one I actually used in September 1998, as you can see from the article on TheStreet.com that I quote in Chapter 4, as I want this record to be as close to the traditional Dow Theory as possible. I left out other more recent signals for the same reason.

APPENDIX B

Capitulation Indicators Detailed Record

I have split the details of the eight capitulation indicators into Tables B.1 and B.2 as they all would not fit on one and still be readable. Since they are related to stock market lows, I have included those dates and market levels to help you judge the validity of each of the indicators.

Author's notes: Data for VIX started in 1993 and was backtested to 1990. My data were live from 1969 and backtested to 1953. "Signal Date" is the first day in the case of multiple signals. Lowry's signals are after at least two "90%" downside days followed by a "90%" upside day or two "80%" upside days, as using just one resulted in considerably more false signals than are shown in the table. The "Days before Low" column is number of calendar days. A (−) is used if before the low, a (+) or no sign if after the low.

Table B.1 Details of Leading Capitulation Indicators

	Bear Market Low	Arms/TRIN		VIX		Lowry's 90%		My Capitulation	
Date	DJ Average S&P 500	Signal Date	Days before Low	Signal Date	Days before Low	Signal Date	Days before Low	Signal Date	Days before Low
6/26/1962	@535.76	Did not exist		Did not exist		11/10/1960	Extraneous	6/22/1962*	−4
Same date	52.32					6/28/1962	2		
Already bull market						10/29/1962	Extraneous		
						6/30/1965	Extraneous		
10/7/1966	744.32	Did not exist		Did not exist		9/12/1966	−25	No signal	
Same date	73.2					10/12/1966	5		
						10/29/1966	22		
						6/6/1967	Extraneous		
						4/8/1968	Extraneous		
5/26/1970	631.16	5/4/1970	−21	Did not exist		5/27/1970	1	5/25/1970	−1
Same date	69.29	10/18/1970	Extraneous						
Already bull market		11/3/1970	Extraneous						
		11/26/1970	Extraneous						
Not bear low		11/18/1970	−18	Did not exist		8/16/1971	Extraneous	8/23/1974	−41
12/6/1974	577.6		36			1/3/1974	False	9/30/1974	−3
10/3/1974	62.28					1/2/1975	27		
						8/28/1975	Extraneous		

(continued)

	DJIA				
Not bear low				1/5/1976	Extraneous
				11/10/1977	False
2/28/1978	742.12	No signal		No signal	No signal
3/5/1978	86.94		Did not exist	11/1/1978	13
(11/14/1978)	92.49			11/26/1979	Extraneous
4/21/1980	759.13	3/24/1980	−3	Did not exist	
3/27/1980	98.22	12/8/1980	Extraneous	3/28/1980	1
				11/12/1980	Extraneous
Already bull market			Extraneous		
Not bear low		8/24/1981	False		
Not bear low		1/5/1982	False		
Not bear low				1/28/1982	False
8/12/1982	776.92	No signal		No signal	No signal
Same date	102.42	10/25/1982	Extraneous		
Already bull market			Extraneous		
		7/7/1986	Extraneous	1/2/1987	Extraneous
		11/18/1986	Did not exist	10/21/1987	2
10/19/1987	1738.74	10/19/1987	0	10/29/1987	10
12/4/1987	223.92	11/30/1987	−4	1/4/1988	31
Already bull market		Did not exist		1/25/1988	Extraneous
				5/31/1988	Extraneous
				5/11/1990	Extraneous
				8/27/1990	−45
10/13/1989		Extraneous		10/19/1987	0
				12/3/1987	−1

Table B.1 (continued)

Bear Market Low		Arms/TRIN		VIX		Lowry's 90%		My Capitulation	
Date	DJ S&P 500	Signal Date	Days before Low	Signal Date	Days before Low	Signal Date	Days before Low	Signal Date	Days before Low
10/11/1990	2365.1	No signal		No signal	n/a	11/12/1990	32	8/23/1990	−49
Same date	295.46								
Already bull market		11/15/1991	Extraneous			4/5/1994	Extraneous		
		10/27/1997	Extraneous			8/2/1996	Extraneous		
		1/9/1998	Extraneous						
8/31/1998	7539.07	8/31/1998	0	8/31/1998	0	9/8/1998	8	8/31/1998	0
Same date	957.28								
Not market low		4/14/2000	False						
		3/13/2001	False						
9/21/2001	8235.81	4/3/2001	False	9/20/2001	−1	No signal		9/20/2001	−1
Same date	965.8	No signal							
Bull market		1/29/2002	Extraneous						
Not market low		4/11/2002	False						
First low				7/23/2002	0			7/19/2002	−4
(7/23/02) of									

double bottom

	Signal 1	Signal 2	Signal 3	Signal 4
10/9/2002 — 7286.3				
Same date — 776.76	9/3/2002 @8308 (−36)	10/7/2002 (−2)	No signal (−154)	10/9/2002 (0)
Bull market	12/27/2002 @8304		3/13/2003 @8141.92	
Bull market	3/4/2003 @7705			
Bear market lows	3/22/2004 Extraneous		3/22/2004 Extraneous	
Identified	6	3† (last 3)	9†	8* (includes last 5)
Missed (No signal):	4(½ of last 8)	1†	4(½ of last 8)	4
Extraneous signals:	13	0	16	0
False signals:	6	0	3	0

*Only one from backtesting.
†All from backtesting.
‡Unknown how many from backtesting.

Table B.2 Results for the Other Four Capitulation Indicators

Bear Market Low		Lows/Total		Put/Call		Inflow/Outflow		200 Day	
Date	DJ Average S&P 500	Signal Date	Days before Low	Signal Date	Days before Low	Date	Days before Low	Date	Days before Low
6/26/1962	@535.76	Did not exist		Did not exist		?		6/21/1962	−5
Same date	52.32								
10/7/1966	744.32	Did not exist		Did not exist		?		No signal	
Same date	73.2								
5/26/1970	631.16	Did not exist		Did not exist		No signal		5/26/1970	0
Same date	69.29								
Already bull market						3/1/1972	Extraneous		
12/6/1974	577.6	Did not exist		Did not exist		No signal			
10/3/1974	62.28							8/29/1974	−35
Already bull market						4/1/1975	Extraneous		
Not bear low						4/1/1977	False		
2/28/1978	742.12	No signal		Did not exist		No signal		No signal	
3/6/1978	86.9								
Not bear low		10/22/1979	False						
4/21/1980	759.13			Did not exist		No signal		No signal	
3/27/1980	98.22	3/7/1980	−20						
Already bull market						6/1/1980	Extraneous		
Not bear low		9/23/1981	False						
8/12/1982	776.92	No signal		Did not exist		No signal		No signal	
Same date	102.42								

Date	Price	Lows/Total		Put/Call		Inflow/Outflow		200 Day	
10/19/1987	1738.74	10/19/1987	0	12/3/1987	-1	10/1/1987	Low spike / Confirmed late Dec +25?	10/20/1987	1
12/4/1987	223.92								
10/11/1990	2365.1	8/17/1990	-55	No signal		8/1/1990	Low spike / Confirmed early Oct -5?	No signal	
Same date	295.46	9/25/1990	-16						
Already bull market		4/4/1994	Extraneous						
8/31/1998	7539.07	8/5/1998	-26	8/21/1998	-10	8/1/1998	Low spike / Confirmed early Oct +36?	No signal	
Same date	957.28	10/8/1998	38	10/8/1998	38				
Not bear low						3/1/2001	False		
9/21/2001	8235.81	9/19/2001	-2	9/17/2001	-4	9/1/2001	Low spike / Confirmed early Nov +46?	9/20/2001	-1
Same date	965.8								
Already bull market				2/15/2002	Extra				
				6/21/2002	-33				
First low (7/23/02)		7/24/2002	-1	7/19/2002	-5	7/2/2002	Low spike / Confirmed early Sep +45?	7/22/2002	-1
of double bottom									
				9/17/2002	-22				
				9/18/2002	-21				
				9/19/2002	-20				
10/9/2002	7286.27	10/10/2002	-1	9/20/2002	-19			9/30/2002	-9
Same date	776.76	5/10/2004	Extraneous						

	Lows/Total	Put/Call	Inflow/Outflow	200 Day
Bear market lows Identified:	6	4	5	6
	(includes last 5)	(includes last 3)	(last 5)	
Missed (no signal):	2	1	5	
Extraneous signals:	2	1	3	0
False signals:	2	0	2	0

APPENDIX C

CPA Verification of the Schannep Indicator

A CPA verification of the Schannep Timing Indicator signals follows that covers the period before my "Market Letter" was open to the public in 1998. Since then it has been monitored by TimerTrac.com and Hulbert Financial Digest of *MarketWatch from Dow Jones.*

> October 16, 1998
> Schannep Timing Indicator, LLC
> To: John D. Schannep, President
> We have performed certain agreed-upon procedures, as discussed below, in connection with your Stock Market Major Trend Timing Indicator. The purpose of this indicator is to identify changes in the trend of price movements on the major stock averages. Our procedures and findings were as follows:
>
> 1. You provided us with a written narrative on the application of your indicator formula. We reviewed this with you in detail to develop a comprehensive understanding of its application. The results of this formula are referred to as signal dates, either to buy or sell based on the expected price movement of the major stock averages. Data used in applying this formula consisted of momentum statistics on the major stock averages and monetary statistics from the Federal Reserve Board.

Our procedures were designed to sample test the signal dates which you obtained with the formula and to compare these dates with actual changes in price movement on the Standard and Poor's Composite and Dow Jones stock averages.

2. We recomputed the buy and sell signal dates from December 31, 1953 through September 16, 1998 using your indicator formula and the required momentum and monetary statistics. The average momentum statistics for the sample dates were published by Dean Witter Reynolds in its "COMPARE" service and kept current in your own computer. The Federal Reserve Board monetary statistics for the sample dates were obtained from the Federal Reserve Bank of St. Louis, the Wall Street Journal, and the internet. Our computations verified the same dates that you arrived at for this period of time. These signal dates are as follows:

Buy Signals	Sell Signals
January 25, 1954	August 20, 1956
May 5, 1958	November 12, 1959
January 3, 1961	May 10, 1962
November 14, 1962	May 2, 1966
December 27, 1966	January 22, 1968
April 11, 1968	March 7, 1969
August 24, 1970	February 23, 1973
October 22, 1973	November 20, 1973
November 4, 1974	October 31, 1977
April 17, 1978	October 26, 1978
June 11, 1980	August 31, 1981
August 23, 1982	February 22, 1984
August 21, 1984	October 16, 1987
March 16, 1988	August 24, 1990
January 25, 1991	June 20, 1994
February 22, 1995	August 27, 1998

3. We then compared all of the signal dates to actual changes in the price indices for two major stock averages, Standard and Poor's Composite and the Dow Jones averages. These comparisons are shown on the attached schedules [not presented]. Schedule A shows actual price movement between

the buy and sell signals. Schedule B shows actual price movement between the sell and buy signals. The indices on these
averages at the sample signal dates were obtained by us from
the Wall Street Journal, the Internet, and the Tucson Public
Library Information Line.

4. This is an update of our report originally completed February
   20, 1985.

Kyle DeFoor, CPA
2930 NORTH SWAN SUITE 209
TUCSON, ARIZONA 85712

APPENDIX D

Complete Record of the Composite Timing Indicator

Whenever a first buy signal of any of the four types occurs, buy to 50 percent invested. If a second *type* of buy occurs, go to fully invested (i.e., add another 50 percent). If the second buy is another capitulation, then add just another 25 percent, adding the final 25 percent when another type of buy signal occurs. If a buy is reversed in time by the same type signal, return to the original position (i.e., if 50 percent was bought, then sell that 50 percent upon a reverse signal occurring).

Whenever a first sell indicator occurs, sell half or 50 percent. Upon a second indicator, sell out 100 percent. **Bold italicized** is first buy or sell; underscored completes 100 percent. I recommend buying *equal* amounts of Diamonds (DIA), Spiders (SPY), and the NYSE i-Shares (NYC) so as to participate fully in the market's advances/declines. Results shown include dividends and interest on cash. Market levels are for the Dow Jones Industrial Average (DJIA). When bull/bear markets become "official" both the DJIA and the Standard & Poor's 500 levels are shown.

The original Dow Theory was used in the twentieth century; thereafter, the Dow Theory for the twenty-first century is used.

Table D.1 Component's Dates and Market Levels of the Composite's Signals with Starting and Ending Investment Results

Capitulation Buy Signal Type Date/Level	Dow Theory %	Dow Theory Buy or Sell Date/Level	Schannep Timing Indicator %	Schannep Buy or Sell Date/Level	Definition of "Official" Bull or Bear met %	Definition of "Official" Bull or Bear met Buy or Sell Date/Level	Signal %	Signal Composite Indicator	Start 12/31/53 $10,000
		B-1/19/54@288.27		B-1/25/54@290.40	50	*Bull:* previously in existence	50	**Average Buy 289.34**	$10,005
	50		**50**			***4/6/56 Bull Market High: 521.05***			$10,081
		S-10/1/56@468.70		S-8/20/56@511.24		*Bear:* 10/17/57@436.87 (S&P@40.65)	n/a	**Average Sell 489.97**	$19,170
	50		50		**50**	***10/22/57 Bear Market Low: 419.79***			$18,502
		B-5/2/58@459.56		B-5/5/58@461.12	50	*Bull:* 7/25/58@501.76 (S&P@46.97)	n/a	**Average Buy 460.34**	$19,335
	50		**50**		**50**	No Bear Market			$28,080
		S-3/3/60@612.05		S-11/12/59@644.26				**Average Sell 628.16**	$27,659
			50						$28,185
		B-10/10/61@706.67		B-1/3/61@610.25	50	***12/13/61 Bull Market High: 734.91***		**Average Buy 658.46**	$30,863
	50		50			*Bear:* 5/25/62@611.88 (S&P@59.47)	n/a	**Average Sell 662.96**	$31,943
		S-4/26/62@678.68		S-5/10/62@647.23	50				$32,039
B-6/22/62@539.19	**50**		**50**						

208

Transaction	Shares	Market Event	Average	Value
B-11/9/62@616.13	50	6/26/62 *Bear Market Low:* 535.76	**Average Buy 577.66**	$37,165
B-11/14/62@630.48 (584.84 average Buy level)	n/a	*Bull:* 11/29/62@652.61 (S&P@62.41)	n/a	
S-5/2/66@931.95	50	2/9/66 *Bull Market High:* 995.15		$64,236
S-5/5/66@899.77	50	*Bear:* 8/22/66@792 (S&P@78.24)	n/a **Average Sell 915.86**	
B-12/27/66@792.20	50	10/7/66 *Bear Market Low:* 744.32		$66,436
B-1/11/67@822.49	50	*Bull:* 4/24/67@887.53 (S&P@92.62)	n/a **Average Buy 807.35**	
S-10/24/67@888.18	**50**			$74,408
S-1/22/68@871.71	50	No Bear Market	**Average Sell 879.95**	$75,152
B-4/11/68@905.69	50			$79,811
B-10/1/68@942.32	50	12/3/68 *Bull Market High:* 985.21	**Average Buy 924.05**	
S-2/25/69@899.80	**50**			$79,332
S-3/7/69@911.18	50	*Bear:* 7/28/69@806.23 (S&P@90.21)	n/a **Average Sell 905.49**	
B-10/27/69@860.28	**50**			$82,902
S-1/26/70@768.88	50	(−10.6% on 1/2)		$79,785
				$81,620
B-5/25/70@641.36	**50**	5/26/70 *Bear Market Low:* 631.16	**Average Buy 670.92**	
B-8/24/70@759.58 (700.47 average Buy level)	50			$97,863

(continued)

Table D.1 (continued)

Capitulation Buy Signal Type Date/Level	%	Dow Theory Buy or Sell Date/Level	%	Schannep Timing Indicator Buy or Sell Date/Level	%	Definition of "Official" Bull or Bear met Buy or Sell Date/Level	%	Signal Composite Indicator	Start 12/31/53 $10,000
		B-9/28/70@758.97	n/a		n/a	*Bull:* 9/4/70@771.15 (S&P@82.83)	n/a		
		S-7/28/71@872.01	**50**			No Bear Market			$130,745
		B-2/10/72@921.28	<u>50</u>	(−5.6% on ½)					$135,452
						1/11/73 Bull Market High:		**1051.7**	
		S-3/23/73@922.71	<u>50</u>	S-2/23/73@959.89	<u>50</u>			**Average Sell 941.30**	$194,373
						Bear: 8/21/73@857.84 (S&P@100.89)	n/a		
				B-10/22/73@960.57	**50**	No Bull Market			
				S-11/20/73@844.90	**50**	(−12.1% on ½)	<u>50</u>		$209,534
									$197,305
				B-11/4/74@657.24 (663.79 average level)	25		<u>25</u>	**Average Buy 660.16**	$211,111
B-8/23/74@686.80	**50**								$224,188
B-9/30/74@603.25	25								
		B-11/5/74@674.75	n/a			**12/6/74 Bear Market Low:** *Bull:* 1/27/75@692.66 (S&P@75.37)	n/a	**577.6**	
						9/21/76 Bull Market High:		**1014.79**	
		S-10/24/77@802.32	**50**						

210

Trade	Qty	Trade	Qty	Market Event	Qty	Average	Value
		S-10/31/77@818.35	50	*Bear:* 1/10/78@781.53 (S&P@90.17)	n/a	**Average Sell 810.34**	$285,615
				2/28/78 Bear Market Low: *742.12*	***50***		
B-6/6/78@866.51	50	B-4/17/78@810.12	50		n/a	**Average Buy 838.32**	$298,468
				Bull: 8/3/78@886.87 (S&P@103.51)			$321,152
S-10/19/78@846.41	50			***9/11/78 Bull Market High:*** *907.74*			
		S-10/26/78@821.12	50	*Bear:* 3/26/80@762.12 (S&P@98.68)	n/a	**Average Sell 833.76**	$325,969
B-5/13/80@816.89	50			***4/21/80 Bear Market Low:*** *759.13*			
		B-6/11/80@872.70	50	*Bull:* 7/14/80@905.55 (S&P@120.01)	n/a	**Average Buy 844.80**	$377,146
				4/27/81 Bull Market High: *1024.05*			$404,677
S-7/2/81@959.19	50	S-8/31/81@881.47	50			**Average Sell 920.33**	$465,783
				Bear: 9/23/81@840.94 (S&P@115.65)	n/a		
				8/12/82 Bear Market Low: *776.92*	***50***		
		B-8/23/82@891.17		*Bull:* 9/3/82@925.13 (S&P@122.68)	50	**Average Buy 908.15**	$521,693
B-10/7/82@965.97	n/a						
S-1/25/84@1231.89	***50***						

(continued)

211

Table D.1 *(continued)*

Capitulation Buy Signal Type Date/Level	Dow Theory %	Dow Theory Buy or Sell Date/Level	Schannep Timing Indicator %	Schannep Buy or Sell Date/Level	Definition of "Official" Bull or Bear met %	Definition Buy or Sell Date/Level	Composite Indicator Signal	Composite %	Start 12/31/53 $10,000
			50	S-2/22/84@1134.21 B-8/21/84@1239.73	50 **50**	No Bear Market	**Average Sell 1183.05**		$705,850
	50	B-1/21/85@1261.37				***8/25/87 Bull Market High:***	**Average Buy 1250.55** **2722.42**		$769,376
	50	S-10/15/87@2355.09	50	S-10/16/87@2246.74	50	*Bear:* 10/16/87@2246.74 (S&P@282.70)	**Average Sell 2300.91**	n/a	$1,471,046
B-10/19/87@1738.74 **50**						***10/19/87 Bear Market Low:***	1738.74		$1,471,526
B-12/3/87@1776.53 25	25	B-1/7/88@2051.89							$1,493,356
			25	B-3/16/88@2064.32 (1853.57 average Buy level)	n/a	*Bull:* 2/29/88@2071.62 (S&P@267.82)	**Average Buy 1826.48**	n/a	$1,680,225
	50	S-10/13/89@2569.26	50	(missed 14.3% on 1½)					$2,486,405
	50	B-6/4/90@2935.19							$2,793,163
	50	S-8/3/90@2809.65	50			***7/16/90 Bull Market High:***	2999.75		$2,689,816

Transaction	%	Signal / Note	Market Event & Level	Avg / Index	Value
B-8/23/90@2483.42 — This capitulation buy reaffirms the 50% invested position and offsets the *Bear* Sell signal and negates the Schannep Timing Indicator		*Bear:* 8/23/90@2483.42 (S&P@307.06)		n/a	$2,541,860
S-8/24/90@2532.92	n'a				
			10/11/90 Bear Market Low:	**2365.1**	
B-12/5/90@2610.40	50			**Average Buy 2772.80 (from 6/4 and 12/5)**	$2,646,222
B-1/25/91@2659.41 (2571.67 average Buy level)	n'a	*Bull:* 2/6/91@2830.94 (S&P@358.07)			
S-6/20/94@3741.90	50	No Bear Market			$4,191,196
B-2/22/95@3973.05	50	(missed 6.2% on ½)			$4,446,240
			7/17/98 Bull Market High:	**9337.97**	
S-8/4/98@8487.31	50			**Average Sell 8326.65**	$7,774,605
S-8/27/98@8165.99	50	*Bear:* 8/31/98@7539.07 (S&P@957.28)		n/a	$7,646,878
B-8/31/98@7539.07	50		**8/31/98 Bear Market Low:**	**7539.07**	
B-11/2/98@8706.50	50			**Average Buy 8122.79**	$7,662,172
B-11/5/98@8915.47 (8227.27 average Buy level)	r/a	*Bull:* 11/6/98@8975.46 (S&P@1141.01)		n/a	
S-8/30/99@10914.14	50	No Bear Market			$10,295,233
S-9/23/99@10318.59	50			**Average Sell 10,621.56**	$9,755,763
B-12/3/99@11286.18	50		**1/14/00 Bull Market high:**	**11,722.98**	$9,849,034

(continued)

Table D.1 (continued)

Capitulation — Buy Signal Type Date/Level	Dow Theory %	Dow Theory — Buy or Sell Date/Level	Schannep Timing Indicator %	Schannep Timing Indicator — Buy or Sell Date/Level	Definition of "Official" Bull or Bear met %	Definition of "Official" Bull or Bear met — Buy or Sell Date/Level	Signal — Composite Indicator	Start 12/31/53 $10,000
					50	S-*Bear:* 3/16/01@9823.41 (S&P@1150.53)		$9,750,535
B-9/20/01@8376.21 (**50**)						**9/21/01 Bear Market Low:**	**8,235.81**	$10,058,953
	50	B-11/6/01@9591.12 (9225.65 average. Buy level) Note: "21st Century" signals start here.					**Average Buy 8800.93**	$10,807,381
						Bull: 11/19/01@9976.46 (S&P500@1151.06)		
					50	**3/19/02 Bull Market High:**	**10635.25**	
		S-6/3/02@9709.79		S-7/3/02@9054.97	n/a	*Bear:* 7/10/02@8813.50 (S&P@920.47)	**Average Sell 9382.38**	$11,629,425
B-7/19/02@8019.26 (**50**)	50	B-8/14/02@8743.31 (8503.13 ave. Buy level) S-9/17/02@8207.55	50					$11,654,673
								$12,281,430
B-10/9/02@7286.27 (25)	25	B-11/4/02@8571.60 (8061.52 average Buy level)	25	B-11/5/02@8678.27 (8116.79 average Buy level)	n/a	**10/9/02 Bear Market Low:**	**7286.27**	$11,710,201
						Bull: 11/21/02@8845.15 (S&P500@933.76)	**Average Buy: 8208.61 (from 8/14, 10/9, and 11/4)**	$11,015,790
								$12,477,849

214

Trade	Shares	Notes		Amount
S-1/24/03@8131.01				$11,916,404
B-4/22/03@8484.99	**50**	No Bear Market		$12,204,962
S-5/10/04@9990.02	**50**	Did not act on this as the Transports saved our bacon (did not go to new lows) but include for the record.		$14,661,546
S-8/5/04@9963.03	25	(Acted on ½ only per e-mail that day as odds were 4 to 1 against a bear market)		$14,520,288
B-11/3/04@10137.05	50			$14,617,727
B-11/22/04 @10489.42	25	No Bear Market		$15,631,630
S-7/12/06@11013.18	**50**			$16,819,856
B-10/12/06 @11947.70	50	No Bear Market		$17,738,578
S-8/14/07@13028.92	**50**			$19,689,125
Actually got a type B-5 Buy signal on 10/5 but eliminated that type Buy from Dow Theory of the twenty-first century unless all three Dow Industrials, Transports, and S&P 500 join in.		*10/9/07 Bull Market High:* **to date**	**14164.53**	
S-1/15/08@12501.11	50	_Bear:_ 3/7/08@11893.69 (S&P 500@1293.37)	**Average Sell: 12765.02**	$19,454,824

215

About the Author

Jack Schannep is a 1956 graduate of the U.S. Military Academy at West Point. For four years he was a jet instructor pilot and academic instructor in the U.S. Air Force. From 1961 until 1968 he was a stockbroker in Phoenix with Dean Witter & Co. (now Morgan Stanley). He opened and managed the Dean Witter Tucson offices from 1968 until retiring as Senior Vice President in charge of the southern Arizona offices in 1984. Jack and his wife, Helen, have three married sons and a married daughter and eight grandchildren, and live in Tucson and Pinetop, Arizona. Jack has been president of numerous civic organizations. He was on the executive committee of the Tucson Chamber of Commerce, was the Arizona state chairman of the National Association of Security Dealers (NASD) Fair Practices Committee, and an allied member of the New York Stock Exchange (NYSE). He has been listed in *Who's Who in America* since 1988.

Jack has had a serious interest in market timing for many years, starting with the Dow Theory nearly 50 years ago. His father-in-law had known Robert Rhea, the great Dow Theorist of the 1930s. In 1962, Jack mimeographed his first market timing letter to his clients. In 1969, he developed a stock market major trend timing indicator. Over the next several years he further developed and improved the indicator. He went from making the necessary calculations on his slide rule and adding machine to his first personal computer 20 years ago. In 1977, at the request of Dean Witter management, he began writing a personal correspondence to his fellow managers, his stockbrokers, and some other colleagues about his advanced market timing indicator and his expectations for the stock market. This became the "Schannep Timing Indicator Quarterly Letter," which Jack continued after his retirement in 1984.

In 1998, Jack opened up his letter to subscribers on the Internet. The Schannep Timing Indicator and The DowTheory.com Newsletter (www.timingindicator.com and/or www.thedowtheory.com) is posted monthly with e-mails to subscribers when there is an indication of capitulation in the market or a change of signal on the Dow Theory, the Schannep Timing Indicator, or the Composite Timing Indicator. Most subscribers are from within the United States, but others live around the world.

Index

SRS   33.6

SICF   67.50

FAZ   11.26